MY FRENCH VUE

MY FRENCH VUE

BISTRO COOKING AT HOME

SHANNON BENNETT

PHOTOGRAPHY BY SIMON GRIFFITHS

SIMON & SCHUSTER
AUSTRALIA

To Madeleine and Phoenix

MY FRENCH VUE: Bistro Cooking at Home
First published in Australia in 2007 by
Simon & Schuster (Australia) Pty Limited
Suite 2, Lower Ground Floor
14-16 Suakin Street
Pymble NSW 2073

A CBS Company
Sydney New York London Toronto

Visit our website at www.simonsaysaustralia.com

Cataloguing-in-Publication data:

Bennett, Shannon.
    My French vue : bistro cooking at home.
    Includes index.
    ISBN 9780731813223 (hbk.).
    1. Cookery, French. I. Griffiths, Simon (Simon John). II.
    Title.

    641.5944

Managing editor: Glenda Downing
Editor: Clare Coney
Cover and internal designer: Natalie Winter
Photographer: Simon Griffiths
Food stylist: Fiona Hammond
Prepress: Graphic Print Group
Printed in China by Phoenix Offset

10 9 8 7 6 5 4 3 2 1

Contents

Introduction

Introduction

Is life about fitting into society? Conforming, bending and moulding around the will of others in order to achieve what we want? The simple answer is 'yes'. Society defines, directs, and sometimes destroys us. But my journey thus far has sought to defy that – seeking the path less travelled to reach my destination.

I take my profession very seriously and it is with great pride that I can say I have achieved all the goals I set out for myself in *My Vue*. Now I have reached them, it seems the goalposts have shifted. While I believe that at Vue de monde I have succeeded in creating a culinary experience that cannot be re-created at home, I now feel it is time to return to where it all began.

It seems to me that the next step in my culinary evolution is to create a book that applies my opinions and ideals about food to everyday life, and brings my knowledge and experience to the daily dinner table and into the home. My ideals have not changed. However, my current challenge is to make those ideals accessible to the family: the cornerstone of any society. If this book can bring one family together to join in creating just one meal a week and so celebrate the joy of a shared table, then I will have succeeded in my mission.

This new purpose in my writing is not about embracing the mundane in dining. One of my principal motivations as a chef and restaurateur has always been to put Melbourne on the global culinary map, and my consistent pursuit of fine dining has meant fighting mediocrity at every turn. Accordingly, I believe the principles of fine dining and an appreciation of the finer things in life can be a regular feature in every household, at every table. This book seeks to make it possible. Education, enthusiasm and a positive attitude can make any goal attainable.

Australia boasts an incredibly high standard and range of produce, of which we should be proud. The challenge now is to be more creative and discerning in our approach to it, remembering always that aspirations to greatness begin in the home. Enjoy!

Shannon Bennett

Food and wine matching

The rituals of matching food and wine are taken much more seriously in European households than they are in Australia, where the wine is often an afterthought. I hope that one day every Australian garners enough interest in and respect for their cooking skills to think about the best wine to serve with the dish they have prepared. Below I have included a rough guide to good matches between varieties of wine and types of food that will help readers make an informed choice.

Lovers of wine in Australia face problems with ensuring their vintages are being stored optimally. Very few homes have good wine cellars, but variations in humidity and inconsistent storage temperatures – both too hot and too cold – can ruin a wine. For a few hundred dollars you will find that a wine storage refrigerator is a great investment.

MEAT

GAME

Goose, pigeon, wild hare and venison are all great served with the Braised Lentils recipe made with lentils du puy, and matched with a Pinot Noir or a cool-climate Shiraz – the wine should have light tannins and an earthy, mushroom-truffle nose. Those who prefer white wine should consider a white Graves from Bordeaux.

Game is often served in a terrine, preserved or salted. With these types of dishes try a Gewürztraminer or an Alsatian-style rich Pinot Gris. There's a great example of this wine produced in Victoria's Mornington Peninsula: T'Gallant's Tribute Pinot Gris.

BEEF

Family meals such as shepherd's pie or meat pies require light red wine like a Beaujolais. Grilled or barbecued steak is perfect with something that has a little more tannin and bigger structure, such as Barossa Valley Shiraz from South Australia; or, if you are like me and prefer lighter, earthier reds, then try a Merlot from Bordeaux.

Chilli and wine is a tough match but I have been surprised by the sweetness a Zinfandel can have on harmonising the flavours of a chilli con carne.

LAMB

Roast meat that has been cooked for a long time and is texturally challenging, like a leg of lamb, is perfectly matched by Rhône wines. A good example of the harmony between them would be to try possibly the most complex recipe in the book, Hay-smoked Lamb, with a rich Rhône Grenache-based wine such as Châteauneuf du Pape.

I have also very much enjoyed the combination of Australian Pinot Noir with lamb stews such as Irish stew or Lancashire hotpot. The heavier, sweeter and slightly fuller-bodied style of Australian pinots enables them to be drunk younger than French ones, and particularly complements these dishes as the heavier flavours are able to cut through their richness.

PORK

Sausages cooked on the barbecue or griddle require a big red like an Australian Shiraz or an American Zinfandel.

Baked ham is a very wine-friendly food; I like it best with unusual wines not normally available in the local bottle shop, such as German or Austrian Pinot Noir or a light vin de pays from the Provence region of south-west France. The Pork Pie recipe on page 65 falls into this category also, because its pastry is very light and delicate.

Spanish or Italian cured hams are best served with wines from their region: Rioja or Chianti Classico Reserva. Pork leg slow-roasted with lemon and garlic also pairs well with Spanish Rioja.

A wine to match roast pork belly should be taken more seriously, particularly with the amount of work that can go into making such a dish, so I would look at spending a little more on the wine and buying a Cabernet blend that has been aged for a few years to soften the tannins and release more intricate aromas and tastes. Many of the world's wine regions have great examples of cabernet blends, such as Bordeaux, Margaret River in Western Australia, Tuscany in Italy and the west coast of the United States.

POULTRY
CHICKEN
I feel that when selecting wine for chicken dishes, there are two ways to go. Chicken that is served simply in salads, or crumbed and fried – such as Chicken Kiev – or is steamed or poached, particularly in Asian-style dishes, is going to be matched well by a wooded Chardonnay. Many great examples of such wines are once again found worldwide, from Australia to Burgundy. One I particularly like is an Italian blend which has a small amount of Sauvignon Blanc added; the Gaja Langhe version is my favourite.

Chicken that has been fricasséed, chicken chasseur, coq au vin or roast chicken are best matched with a fuller-bodied wine, such as Gamay, or even a well-made rosé. Again, there of plenty of great examples on the market.

DUCK AND OTHER POULTRY
Duck, goose, guinea fowl, quail, turkey all fall into a unique category. Most consumers perceive them as game, but true game is wild and these are all farmed; their flavours are milder than those of game. I would generalise by saying that Pinot Noir will suit most dishes, although duck with sweet sauces such as cherry can be well complemented by sweet Alsatian white wines.

FISH
Thai fish cakes, red mullet, mackerel, salmon, tuna and sardines all need dry crisp whites with plenty of fresh zesty acidity to cut the rich oiliness of the aftertaste. Young New World Riesling fits this bill well, most notably from the Frankland River region of southern Western Australia. Rosé is an alternative that can be quite pleasant with these fish, particularly if they are being eaten cold.

SHELLFISH
Crab, langoustines, lobster, mussels and oysters are classical friends of white burgundy, and the more simply the dish is prepared then the better the wine will enhance it. French Chablis without any oak influence is my favourite match. For more complex dishes go for heavier, oak-influenced Chardonnay, and when you serve a bouillabaisse that may have a touch of spice then lean towards a heavier style of rosé that is well chilled.

VEGETARIAN

Salads and asparagus are best served with herbaceous wines like unoaked Sauvignon Blanc which has a very grassy nose. Both asparagus and hollandaise sauce seem to complement Sauvignon Blanc very well. Tomato-based pasta dishes need a Chianti. Quiche served cold is best with a Riesling but when hot is best with a Côtes du Rhône. Condrieu – or an Australian version made from the Viognier grape, with its honeysuckle aroma and viscous, oily texture – go well with mayonnaise-based salads. Vegetable-based broths and light soups without cream or butter are best suited to a Spanish sherry.

Egg dishes are very difficult to match with wine, because egg has a very thick texture. I find that Champagne is lean enough to wash eggs down, leaving a lovely nutty lemon finish.

Mushrooms and earthy ingredients need an earthy wine like Gamay or Pinot Noir, or even an Italian Dolcetto. However, Vue de monde's much-loved truffle risotto seems to be made for Pinot Gris and we have consistently served this match for the last seven years.

CHEESE

Stilton, Roquefort and soft to medium blue cheeses all are well complemented by port and sweet Madeira-style wines – hence the recipe for Roquefort with Chocolate Sponge on page 189, as the chocolate sponge makes even a greater bridge between the wine. Sauternes is also a suitable match with blue cheese, particularly a firmer blue like Stilton.

Goat's cheese, such as a well-matured Crottin, is said to be iconic with Sauvignon Blanc but I disagree, believing that Viognier is a far more enjoyable match – but I will let you be the judge of this.

Aged brie is always best served with late-harvest Alsatian varieties such as Gewürztraminer, Riesling or Pinot Gris. From here on, cheese and wine matching is pretty straightforward. Cheddar and gruyère are best served with a heavy white, such as Condrieu or Gewürztraminer. Pinot Noir, Bordeaux or a red Côtes du Rhône bring out the best characteristics of Italian Grana Padano parmesan.

DESSERTS AND SWEETS

Chocolate-based desserts have powerful cloying textures and flavours and therefore require a fortified wine such as Rutherglen Muscat from north-east Victoria, a Portuguese port, sweet Madeira or even maple whisky, a Canadian liqueur.

Lemon tarts and other fruit-based desserts need to be linked with citrus-style wines, particularly Riesling, and especially those from Germany: Auslese or the more extravagant but amazing Beerenauslese. The Australian late-harvest Rieslings are improving in quality each year; look out for the Mount Horrocks Cordon Cut Riesling as the best example from this region.

Puff pastry dishes with cream need a buttery Chardonnay, normally meaning one that has been matured for quite some time in oak. In contrast, crème brûlée and soufflé have strong sweet textures and are well matched by a botrytis-style wine from Sauternes. Cakes that contain alcohol, such as trifle, need the upfront hit of that alcohol matched with a wine made the same way; the Italian Vin Santo is a good option.

✦

I hope this guide is of some use when matching food and wine. You should also use the knowledge of your local wine merchant: ask for information on new arrivals and vintage recommendations. Your wine merchant may also be able to fulfil a special request for a back-dated vintage of a wine you really like, as most importers store bin ends from older vintages – this can add an extra dimension to a meal, as simple food can be made into an amazing feast with the right wine.

Basic ingredients

In this section I cover items that you should always have in the pantry, freezer or refrigerator. I use these ingredients in the recipes in this book. If you don't have a lot of time but are passionate about what you are going to eat then the following items will allow you to cook most of my basic recipes. Make an effort over the next month to build up your stocks of these items. Take note of particular brands if I recommend, as these will have been chosen carefully and are based on my research in my own home.

This is by no means a definitive list and does not include necessities to cater for a regular family seven days per week, but it does summarise useful ingredients. There is nothing worse than starting a dish and finding out you don't have a vital ingredient in the cupboard.

THE PANTRY

AAA BAKERS' FLOUR Strong plain (all purpose) flour. The flour has not been milled as fine as ordinary plain flour. AAA bakers' flour is the ideal flour for making pasta at home. Please note that soft bakers' flour is required for baking certain cakes and biscuits; this is found in many brands but in the industry there is a standard name, which is T55. If strong plain flour is not available standard plain flour will suffice.

ANCHOVIES (Ortiz) I put these in everything from mayonnaise to caper butter that accompanies fried fish. No other brand comes close to the quality of Ortiz anchovies.

BREADCRUMBS, JAPANESE PANKO Panko is a type of breadcrumb available in all good Asian stores. The crumbs are large, light, white and flaky. Panko crumbs make the best crispy oysters around. The second-best option, if panko are not available, is to make your own by drying some white bread in a very low oven (the lowest it can go) and then blending in the food processor until very fine.

CALVADOS Add to apple when making apple pie or marinate pork chops in it before grilling, or simply deglaze the pan with it when making a jus or gravy from roast pork or lamb.

CIDER Add to roast potatoes and braised pork halfway through the roasting process and cover the tray tightly with aluminium foil, or add at the last minute to a sauce. It's a great addition to apple purée when serving it with pheasant or pork.

CINNAMON Whole sticks or quills are better than ground spice because they keep longer.

CORNICHONS Miniature gherkins, firm and small. They are much used in France and you should look out for French brands. I cannot stand the large spongy gherkins that are normally over-sweetened. Cornichons are great on their own or added to salads, sauces and dressing.

GELATINE, TITANIUM Gelatine in leaf form comes in various types: bronze, silver, gold, platinum and titanium. It's confusing. Gelatine has no world standard when it comes to weight setting strength (bloom) so I use titanium in all my recipes. Leaf gelatine tends to be stocked only by specialist food and kitchen supply shops. There is usually no labelling information whatsoever regarding its setting powers, so stick to titanium. Powdered gelatine is in every supermarket, usually with gelling strength indicated, which will help if you are trying to convert quantities.

GREEN PEPPERCORNS IN BRINE If you have never made nor tried pepper steak then you must cook it: the recipe for Green Peppercorn Sauce is on pages 124–5. Another favourite way of using green peppercorns is in duck confit with peppercorn sauce. Once the container is opened the peppercorns will last for months in an airtight container in the refrigerator.

GROUND ALMONDS Available in most grocery stores and used extensively in dessert bases, they will keep in an airtight container for several months.

HARICOT BEANS, DRIED OR CANNED Essential in cassoulet, but also great when puréed and seasoned with olive oil and white truffle oil.

LENTIL DU PUY When you have tried this variety of lentil you will never go back to ordinary ones. These tiny green pulses have the best flavour. Read more about them on page 160.

MADRAS CURRY POWDER Good for making oils and seasoning fish and prawns.

MINIATURE CAPERS (LILLIPUT) Sometimes these are hard to find. They are small yet have a very strong mature taste and they are more texturally satisfying than the larger, softer capers normally found in recipes.

MURRAY RIVER SALT This should be the most used salt in your cupboard. Its flavour is amazingly concentrated and it dissolves very quickly. The salt is not artificially bleached – it is a light pink – and using it helps the environment in a very small way, by removing salt from our inland river system. I would also like to say that adding salt to water whilst cooking vegetables does not flavour the vegetables, but it does shorten the cooking time. Potato is the only vegetable where adding salt has a positive effect on the flavour.

OIL, EXTRA-VIRGIN OLIVE This is the oil I use to drizzle over salads, fish and roasted meats.

OIL, OLIVE For deep or shallow frying I use plain olive oil, which lasts longer than extra-virgin and the flavour is cleaner.

OIL, VEGETABLE A very neutral flavour that is good for mayonnaise.

OLIVES I suggest your cupboard contains two types. Both are great for eating but the Spanish black Empeltre variety is also good for drying and I use it in the recipe for Spanish Ham with Marinated Tomatoes (page 28), while my favourite eating olive is the small green Arbequina, also from Spain. Occasionally I have seen Victorian wild olives in providores: they are small and vary in colour within each jar. I recommend buying these when you spot them. They are mainly harvested around the Grampians region of Victoria.

SAFFRON Used in a lot of Provençal-style dishes. Indian saffron is the most commonly available. A small amount is all that is needed, so do not be put off by the price.

SHERRY VINEGAR The Spanish De Soto brand is the best all-purpose vinegar. There is something about using sherry vinegar when finishing a sauce or dressing that produces a result other vinegars don't. For a simple dressing try mixing 1 tablespoon sherry vinegar with 3 tablespoons walnut oil and spoon this over steamed baby potatoes, still in their skins, split in two and seasoned with Murray River salt.

SUGAR Caster (superfine) is the best all-round sugar to keep. Madagascar is the best producer in the world of quality sugar and it is a treat to have some brown Madagascan sugar for a good cup of coffee.

SULTANAS SOAKED IN BRANDY Great served with cheese, and added to baked custards. Simply put 4 cups of sultanas in 4 cups of brandy and leave in a sterilised, airtight jar for 2 weeks to mature.

TOMATOES, CANNED Any Italian brand is good enough; but make sure they are whole tomatoes. Fresh tomatoes are always best, but a good canned brand will get you through the colder months and save you precious preparation time; I would rather used canned tomatoes than ones grown hydroponically out of season.

TUNA, CANNED Great in sauces, salads and in pastas. The Serena brand is a well-known favourite worldwide.

VUE DE MONDE EIGHT-SPICE POWDER A recipe for this is on page 21. The powder is essential in quite a few recipes but it is also great churned into ice-cream, added to tarts and even spicing roast meats. Store it in an airtight jar.

WALNUT OIL Great added to the pan juices of roast chicken, but it has many other uses.

THE FREEZER

BOUILLABAISSE STOCK How many times have you thrown away prawn shells, fish heads and bones? Well, no longer! You are going to keep them: put them in freezer bags, freeze them and when you have accumulated around 1 kg make a beautiful rich red stock. Then freeze the stock in 500 ml (1 pint) batches to make bouillabaisse risotto.

BROAD BEANS These freeze surprisingly well. I either make them into a purée or serve them tossed in butter or olive oil to accompany pasta or meats. They are great to have around.

BROWN CHICKEN STOCK Follow the recipe on page 17 and freeze in 500 ml (1 pint) batches. The stock is invaluable: I serve it with grilled steak and braised pork belly. Also great served with steamed white-fleshed fish like snapper by mixing 3 tablespoons stock, 1 tablespoon of browned butter and 1 tablespoon of sherry vinegar, spoon over fish and serve.

CHICKEN STOCK Follow the recipe on page 17. Keep in 500 ml (1 pint) portions, frozen, for all sorts of requirements. Make a large batch every few months and freeze it. You can also use the carcass from a roast chicken to make a stock.

FISH STOCK No explanation is needed, it's just good to have on hand, as you never know when you will need it for a fish recipe.

PEAS The frozen variety is not as good as the fresh but does make a good substitute in sauces and purées.

PUFF PASTRY A 1 kg (2 lb) frozen block of pastry is an essential occupant of any freezer. I recommend cutting the block into quarters, of about 250 g (8 oz) each, for faster and more convenient use. For readers of this book in Australia there is a brand of pastry called Carême which is found in superior supermarkets and has been used in the testing of this book with great results.

TARRAGON I am amazed at how well this herb freezes; it keeps both its colour and flavour. Simply pick and blanch the tarragon in boiling water then refresh in iced cold water, squeeze the leaves dry and wrap in small balls in cling film. Freeze for up to 6 months. To use, chop finely whilst it is still frozen.

VANILLA BEAN ICE-CREAM Vanilla bean ice-cream can accompany any dessert so always have some handy.

VEAL GLAZE This is veal stock that has been reduced, normally by two-thirds, to form a very gelatinous, strong-flavoured glaze. It is used to finish sauces and is added to a roasting tray at the last minute. Keep in 50 ml (2 fl oz) blocks: 1 block will serve 4.

THE FRUIT AND VEGETABLE BASKETS

Not much explanation is needed for these basic items but remember to buy fresh, and from good greengrocers where possible or farmers' markets. Taste is always the

best indicator when looking for the best: a carrot should have taste.

BAY LEAVES Always use fresh. It's a particularly good investment to buy a tree as they grow well in pots and look lovely in the garden.

BROWN SHALLOTS (ESCHALOTS) These are not as strong as onions so are great eaten raw and for finishing salads and sauces. Do not confuse them with baby onions which are much rounder and more pungent in aroma and taste. Two types of shallots are commonly found – the banana shallot and the common shallot – but they taste the same. Asian grocery stores always stock them.

CARROTS Do not buy them too large as they will be woody and dry. Never store in the refrigerator and when they start to shrivel or become flexible throw them away.

GARLIC Buy it fresh with large cloves. Look out for spring garlic, which has a slight green tinge to it; this is great confited in duck fat until tender then served with roast fish.

LEMONS Meyer lemons are my personal favourite. This variety is mainly grown in southern Queensland. It has a yellow-orange skin and slightly lower acidity than other types. Lemon dishes made with Meyers have an extra-zesty flavour which makes them ideal for tarts, cakes and soufflés.

ONIONS Medium-sized brown, white and red are used in this book.

ORANGES Seville oranges are the best for cooking. By the way, never judge an orange by its cover – always smell and taste before deciding.

POTATOES (FRYING) Most potatoes are not harvested during the winter months of July and August and therefore growers store excess potatoes to supply this time of year. Potatoes stored for long periods of time convert the starch inside to simple sugars and therefore when these potatoes are fried they colour very rapidly and cannot achieve a proper crispness. The following are my chosen varieties for different times of the year:

August–April: Spunta

April–September: Desiree from South Australia or large washed from supermarkets

September–December: Redbacks or King Edwards from Western Australia.

POTATOES (KIPFLER) Australia's version of the French ratte potato, grown in rich red soil and very waxy yellow texture. Kipflers are great for steaming and roasting – they won't roast until crisp but do have great flavour and absorb a lot of the roasting juices.

THYME Fresh and green, always buy small amounts weekly.

THE REFRIGERATOR

BUFFALO MOZZARELLA There is no substitute for something that is handmade and no other mozzarella melts the same creamy way. Available in all good markets. The only downside of using buffalo mozzarella is that it is not cheap.

BUTTER, CULTURED Most butter isn't cultured, but good French butter is. The best way to describe cultured butter is whipped fromage blanc that is churned into butter. I still have not found any Australian butter that is as good as that from Normandy. A good substitute for French butter is the Danish Lurpak brand found in most supermarkets.

CELERY A key ingredient in mirepoix for stock.

CREAM, DOUBLE This is used in a few dessert recipes in this book but a carton of it never goes astray as it can be used to accompany tarts and fresh poached fruit. In Australia it is known as double cream or clotted cream.

DIJON MUSTARD An essential condiment for grilled steak and a key ingredient in so many recipes.

EGGS I use large, 60 gram free-range eggs. Older egg whites make stronger meringues so remember to freeze any excess egg whites. Always look for bright yellow yolks and well-formed eggs. When cracked on to a plate the egg white should not run over the surface, but sit on it to a depth of a couple of millimetres: this is the test of a fresh egg.

FENNEL Thinly shaved fennel transforms any salad.

GOOSE OR DUCK FAT To make your own, order some skins of duck or geese from your butcher. Render them down in a heavy pot over a low heat – this will take 3–4 hours and the skins will at first seem to be boiling but once the juices have evaporated a clear, very aromatic oil will appear. When the skins have become golden and shrunk to about a fifth of their original size, strain the fat, cool it and store in the refrigerator in airtight containers, or freeze for long-term storage. Good providores do sell duck fat in 500 g tins; do not be put off by the price as the flavour of a confit made with it is indescribable.

GRANA PADANO The base cheese for all my risotto recipes.

GRUYERE In Australia we are blessed with a fantastic gruyère produced in Tasmania: Heidi Gruyère. I use it both as a table cheese and as a key ingredient in my herb and cheese crusts.

MILK, ORGANIC FULL-CREAM Remember the milk bottles with cream clogging the top? I don't but I have been told about it! When it comes to milk we have lost our way: we drink too much of it, look for excuses to consume more of it. To produce more milk farmers are encouraged to feed their cows with supplements, which can't be good for the cows or the quality of the milk. Supermarkets want the milk to last as long as possible, and to come in low-fat varieties, with added calcium, with vitamins … Have we gone nuts? Organic milk has a wonderful flavour not found in homogenised brands.

Make a vanilla anglaise with full-cream organic milk and you will know what I'm talking about.

OYSTER SAUCE Asian oyster sauce used to finish off a sauce or stir fry; it adds that extra touch.

PARSLEY It's not French if it does not contain parsley.

PISTACHIO PASTE I love pistachio – if you have not yet noticed by visiting my restaurant Vue de monde, where I always have it somewhere on the menu, whether it be flavouring a chicken mousse wrapped around venison or flavouring a crème brûlée. Sevarome is a French brand of pistachio paste available in 500 g tins from good providores. It will keep in an airtight container for 6 months and over that lifespan a $45 tin is good value.

TAHINI PASTE An essential ingredient in baba ghanoush – I make baba ghanoush on impulse as kids love it and it makes a great dip.

TAHITIAN VANILLA BEANS The best variety of vanilla bean in the world: it is plump, soft and big. Sure, Tahitian beans are expensive but their yield and flavour is amazing. The reason they cost so much is that a few years ago Coca-Cola bought 60 per cent of the world's supply, for their Vanilla Coke, forcing the price up by a huge amount.

WINE Any wine that is left over, just push the cork in and keep it in the fridge to be used for the next sauce or marinade.

YUZU JUICE This is increasingly easy to find. It's a citrus fruit, and I use the juice for marinating fish and making dressings. I love the stuff! It is also great to add to homemade lemonade. The juice can be bought frozen or bottled – I have never seen the fresh yuzu fruit in Australia. A good substitute is lemonade fruit.

Basic recipes

HOW TO POACH AN EGG PERFECTLY

1   Bring 1 litre (2 pints) of water to the boil in a saucepan, add a pinch of salt and 1 teaspoon white vinegar and return to the boil, then turn down to a gentle simmer.

2   Crack the eggs into individual cups.

3   Using a whisk or a spoon, stir the water in the saucepan to form a whirlpool. Add the eggs one after the other into the swirling water. Cook for 2–3 minutes for soft poached eggs.

MAYONNAISE

3 egg yolks
1 tablespoon Dijon mustard
2½ tablespoons sherry vinegar
Salt and pepper
300 ml (10 fl oz) sunflower oil
100 ml (3½ fl oz) extra-virgin olive oil
1 tablespoon warm water (optional)
Juice of ½ lemon

1   Combine the egg yolks, mustard, vinegar and seasoning in a food processor. While the motor is running, very slowly pour in a little of the vegetable oil until half has been incorporated.

2   Drizzle in the remaining oil in a thin stream until incorporated. Add a little warm water if the mayonnaise gets too thick.

3   Season with a squeeze of lemon juice.

FRENCH VINAIGRETTE
MAKES 1 CUP

This can be stored in the refrigerator for 1–2 months, or at room temperature for up to 2 weeks.

1 tablespoon Dijon mustard
1 garlic clove, crushed
50 ml (2 fl oz) Champagne vinegar
200 ml (7 fl oz) olive oil
1 tablespoon chopped curly-leaf parsley

Whisk all ingredients together and store in an airtight bottle. Use as required.

BEARNAISE SAUCE

6 egg yolks
100 ml (3½ fl oz) white wine vinegar
800 ml (28 fl oz) clarified butter, melted and
    still warm
Juice of ½ lemon
1 tablespoon chopped tarragon
Salt and pepper

Put the yolks in a bowl over a pan of simmering water. Add vinegar and whisk until yolks are pale and fluffy. Remove from heat. Slowly add butter in a gentle stream, whisking continuously until a thick consistency. Add lemon juice and tarragon and season to taste. Cover bowl with cling film and set aside in a warm place until required.

TUNA MAYONNAISE

3 egg yolks plus 1 whole egg
400 ml (13 fl oz) grapeseed oil
2 tablespoons Champagne vinegar seasoned
    with salt
Juice of 1 lemon
125 g (4 oz) canned tuna, drained and finely
    chopped
4 gherkins, finely chopped
1 tablespoon capers, finely chopped
7 leaves of gelatine

1 Whisk egg yolks and egg together. Slowly incorporate oil, stirring constantly. Add vinegar, lemon juice, tuna, gherkins and capers.

2 Steep gelatine leaves in cold water to soften. Drain and squeeze out any residual water, then microwave for about 15–25 seconds, or until warm and runny. Stir gelatine into mayonnaise.

3 Tightly line a 30 x 20 x 2 cm (12 x 8 x ¾ in) flat tray with cling film. Pour in mayonnaise and smooth off with a palette knife. The mayonnaise should be about 1.5–2 cm (½ – ¾ in) deep. Cover with cling fim and refrigerate until set, then transfer to the freezer.

VEAL STOCK

MAKES 2.5 LITRES (5 PINTS)

1 kg (2 lb 3 oz) veal knuckle bones
500 ml (1 pint) olive oil
1 head of garlic, cut in half
¼ bunch of thyme
5 white peppercorns
1 large carrot, roughly chopped
1 brown onion, roughly chopped
1 celery stalk, roughly chopped
200 g (7 oz) tomato paste
500 ml (1 pint) red wine

1 Preheat the oven to 200°C (400°°°F).

2 Heat a baking tray in the oven for 10 minutes, add the veal bones and half the olive oil and roast for 40 minutes or until dark brown and caramelised.

3 Heat remaining olive oil in a heavy-based frying pan, add the garlic, thyme, peppercorns, carrot, onion and celery and cook for 15 minutes or until coloured and soft. Add the tomato paste and cook, stirring constantly, until a deep brown colour. (This is a crucial stage of the stock: use plenty of oil to prevent the paste burning.) Add red wine and reduce until evaporated.

4 Put the veal bones in a large stockpot and cover with cold water. Bring to the boil and skim off impurities that rise to the surface. Add the vegetable and wine reduction. Bring to the boil and skim off the red fat that rises to the top. Simmer over very low heat for 24 hours, continuously topping up with water to keep the bones covered.

5 Carefully strain through a coarse sieve, then a fine sieve. Return to the stove and reduce by half, skimming any impurities that rise to the surface. Strain once more, allow to cool, and store in the refrigerator or freezer until required.

CHICKEN STOCK

MAKES 2 LITRES (4 PINTS)

5 kg (11 lb) chicken wings
5 litres (10 pints) cold water, to cover
1 large carrot, roughly chopped
1 large leek, roughly chopped
1 large onion, roughly chopped
1 celery stalk, roughly chopped
1 head of garlic, peeled
1 bunch of thyme
1 bay leaf
10 white peppercorns

1 Put the chicken wings in a large stockpot and cover with the water. Bring to the boil, skimming any impurities that rise to the surface. Reduce the heat to low and simmer for 5 minutes, constantly skimming. Add the carrot, leek, onion, celery, garlic, thyme, bay leaf and peppercorns.

2 Continue to skim the surface on a constant basis, removing any oil or fat. Simmer for 7–8 hours. Do not replenish with water, as this will dilute the flavour and texture of the stock.

3 Pass through a fine chinois and cool down as quickly as possible. Use as required.

BROWN CHICKEN STOCK

MAKES 1 LITRE (2 PINTS)

2½ tablespoons olive oil
1 kg (2 lb 3 oz) chicken wings
2 litres (4 pints) Chicken Stock (see previous recipe)
3 shallots, thinly sliced
3 garlic cloves, thinly sliced
4 sprigs of thyme
2 bay leaves
10 white peppercorns

1 Preheat the oven to 180°C (350°F).

2 Put the oil in a shallow baking pan, add the chicken wings and roast in the oven for 20 minutes or until golden.

3 Drain the fat from the pan and discard.

4 Combine the wings with the remaining ingredients in a heavy-based stockpot. Bring to the boil over high heat, then reduce heat to low and simmer for about 2 hours.

5 Strain through a coarse sieve, then through a fine sieve. Allow to cool. Store in an airtight container in the refrigerator for up to 5 days, or freeze for up to 1 month.

HOW TO PEEL
AND DICE A TOMATO

MAKES 2 TABLESPOONS

Where the diced tomato is being used to garnish a dish, rather than as an ingredient in a recipe, for an extra touch of flavour add a teaspoon each of finely diced shallots and finely sliced chives to the dice, and season it with extra-virgin olive oil, Murray River salt and freshly ground pepper.

1 litre (2 pints) water
1 roma (plum) tomato or a vine-ripened tomato
500 ml (1 pint) water cooled with a handful of ice

1   Bring water to the boil over a high heat.

2   Using a sharp paring knife remove the top outer stem of the tomato. At the other end of the tomato, cut a cross approximately 2 cm (¾ in) long. Be gentle, being careful not to embed the knife more than a few millimetres under the skin.

3   Plunge the tomato into the boiling water for 30 seconds. Using a slotted spoon remove and plunge the tomato immediately into the iced water, leave for 3–4 minutes.

4   Using the same knife peel the skin away from the flesh. Discard the skin. Cut the tomato lengthways into quarters and discard the seeds. Pat the chopping board dry with absorbent paper then proceed to dice the tomato into 5 x 5 mm (¼ x ¼ in) pieces.

5   Use as required.

TOMATO FONDUE

1 kg (2 lb 3 oz) tomatoes, roughly chopped
4 garlic cloves, crushed
2 teaspoons white peppercorns, finely crushed
2½ tablespoons extra-virgin olive oil
2 tablespoons sea salt
2 bay leaves
¼ bunch of thyme

1   Preheat the oven to 120°C (250°F).

2   Purée the tomatoes in a food processor; add the garlic, pepper, olive oil and salt and blitz again. Pour mixture into a deep-sided baking tray. Tie the bay leaves and thyme together with some kitchen twine to form a bouquet garni, add to the purée.

3   Bake in the oven for 2 hours or until the tomato fondue is deep red in colour and all moisture has evaporated. Discard the bouquet garni.

4   Push the tomato fondue through a fine sieve.

5   Store in an airtight container in the refrigerator for up to 2 weeks. Suitable for freezing.

Many recipes call for diced tomato, or, as it is sometimes called, tomato concasse.

EIGHT-SPICE POWDER

20 g (¾ oz) juniper berries
30 g (1 oz) whole star anise
15 g (½ oz) white peppercorns
15 g (½ oz) cinnamon quills
15 g (½ oz) cloves
Pinch of saffron threads
25 g (¾ oz) salt
10 g (⅓ oz) cardamom pods

1 Grind all the spices to a fine powder in a spice grinder.

2 Toast the ground spices in a large pan over a medium heat. Allow to cool.

3 Store in an airtight container and use as required.

BOUQUET GARNI

A small bunch of herbs, classically 2 bay leaves, 3–5 parsley stalks, 3 sprigs of thyme and 10 peppercorns, wrapped in a leek leaf, cheesecloth or tied with a piece of string. Ideal for flavouring soups, stews and stocks during cooking, a bouquet garni is removed before serving.

SESAME SALTED FRENCH TOAST
SERVES 4

4 tablespoons sesame seeds
1 tablespoon Murray River salt
4 thick slices sourdough bread
2 tablespoons olive oil
2 eggs, beaten

1 Using a mortar and pestle, grind the sesame and salt together until the salt is no longer visible as flakes and the seeds have been crushed.

2 Turn the grill on to high. Toast one side of the bread until golden. Cut slices into fingers or soldiers.

3 Brush beaten egg on the untoasted side of the bread and then liberally sprinkle sesame salt over it. Toast until golden.

PIZZA DOUGH

MAKES 1 LARGE PIZZA

1.1 kg (2 lb 3½ oz) spelt flour, sifted
50 g (2 oz) olive oil
2 tablespoons fresh yeast
25 g (1 oz) salt
2 teaspoons sugar
5 g (¼ oz) gluten
560 ml (18 fl oz) water

Combine all ingredients in a mixer bowl and work the dough with a dough hook for 15 minutes. The more elastic it becomes, the better. Transfer to a large, lightly oiled container, cover with cling film and set aside in a warm place for 40 minutes or until doubled in size. Knead on a floured surface for 5 minutes, then roll out dough and use immediately.

CONFIT DUCK LEGS

SERVES 4

4 duck legs
1 tablespoon sea salt
Pinch of Eight-Spice Powder (see page 21)
4 sprigs of thyme
1 bay leaf
500 g (1 lb 2 oz) goose fat
Salt and freshly ground pepper

1 Wash the duck legs and pat dry. Cover them with the sea salt, eight-spice powder, thyme and the bay leaf. Refrigerate for 24 hours.

2 Wash the legs under cold running water and pat dry.

3 Preheat the oven to 140°C (275°F).

4 Put 1 tablespoon of the goose fat in a heavy-based frying pan, add the duck legs and brown on both sides over medium heat.

5 Heat the remaining goose fat in a heavy-based baking tray, put the duck legs into the goose fat and place in the oven for 2½ hours to confit; when the duck is ready the meat should start to fall away from the bone.

6 Drain and refrigerate the duck legs for a minimum of 2–3 hours.

Appetisers

SPANISH HAM WITH MARINATED TOMATO

Iberico ham, as it is known in good providores, has until recently been banned from Australian shelves but the curing process now meets quarantine requirements, which is very fortunate for us gourmands. Iberico is a type of serrano ham, which means 'from the mountains'; the cool dry mountain air produces perfect conditions for the curing process. There are three grades of ham and these vary dramatically in price but none are cheap; in my opinion, if price is an issue, I recommend buying a good local Italian prosciutto-style ham instead. For those who are not budget conscious go for jamón ibérico de bellota, which comes from a long-legged type of Iberian black pig fattened on acorns (*bellota* in Spanish), which give a very nutty characteristic to the flavour. This variety is marked with a red band.

100 g (3½ oz) pitted black olives
100 ml (3½ fl oz) extra-virgin olive oil
20 cherry tomatoes
3 garlic cloves, peeled and finely sliced
8 slices Iberico ham
4–5 sprigs of fresh thyme
Salt
Additional 50 ml (2 fl oz) extra-virgin olive oil
1 baguette
25 g (1 oz) baby basil shoots

1   Preheat the oven to 120°C (250°F). Line an oven tray with silicon or baking paper. Place the olives on the tray. Put in the oven for 3–4 hours or until dried. This process may be completed the day before you intend to serve the dish.

2   Put the dried olives in a blender or coffee grinder and blitz to a powder. Drizzle the 100 ml (3½ fl oz) of olive oil into the blender and blitz to combine, resulting in a black olive oil. Pour into a sterilised bottle and set aside.

3   Place a pan of water, about 1 litre (2 pints), on the stove and bring to the boil.

4   Using a small paring knife cut a cross at the top of each cherry tomato. When water is boiling, blanch the tomatoes in the water for 10 seconds then remove and put straight into iced water. Remove after 5 minutes and dry on absorbent paper.

5   Remove the tomatoes' skin. Put peeled tomatoes on a baking tray. Season each with 1 fine slice of garlic, a few leaves of fresh thyme and salt. Drizzle with the remaining extra-virgin olive oil and leave to sit in a warm place for 3 hours, such as a cupboard above an oven.

6   Roughly tear bread into 2 cm (¾ in) cubes and shallow-fry them in olive oil over a medium heat in a heavy-based frying pan. When they are golden, drain on absorbent paper using a slotted spoon.

7   Put 2 slices of the ham (about 50 g/2 oz per person) on to each plate and scatter 5 cherry tomatoes per plate, a few pieces of fried bread and basil, and finish with a good drizzle of the black olive oil.

Pinot Gris is
the perfect wine to
accompany this ...

COLD DUCK SAUSAGE

SERVES 6

I must credit the original of this recipe to Tetsuya Wakuda, as I originally found it in his book *Tetsuya* a number of years ago and have slowly adapted it to my needs. Cold sausage is so versatile. My favourite adaptation of this recipe is to gently fry or grill the sausage so it is warm, then gently fry an egg and place it on top and serve it with a freshly toasted slice of brioche. Another slightly more elaborate serving suggestion is to serve it on top of a warm potato salad with mustard butter sauce.

100 g (3½ oz) coarsely minced chicken
100 g (3½ oz) coarsely minced pork
600 g (1 lb 5 oz) duck mince
Zest of 1 orange
3 tablespoons goose fat
5 tablespoons soy sauce
1 tablespoon chopped tarragon
1 tablespoon chopped rosemary
Salt and pepper
1 teaspoon ground ginger
4 teaspoons Grand Marnier

1 Put all ingredients in a bowl and mix very well. Leave in refrigerator for 24 hours to allow the flavours to infuse.

2 Remove mixture from the bowl and divide into 3–4 portions. Shape these into sausages and wrap them in cling film, making sure it is very tight, and then wrap in aluminium foil.

3 Poach in water at a slow simmer, 90°C (195°F), for 35 minutes. Remove and leave to cool, then refrigerate.

4 To serve, remove foil and plastic, slice to a desired thickness with a sharp knife and serve with a nice pickle and crisp, warm toast.

PRAWN COCKTAIL

They say you should never say 'never' … Ironically, I said that I would never put a prawn cocktail on a menu. Working in London in the mid-1990s changed all that. I now include it on my menu and in this book, attributing the dish to growing up as a chef and realising that perfection is simplicity, and simplicity is a prawn cocktail. Always ensure only the best ingredients are used in this dish and that means fresh green prawns; Crystal Bay prawns are farmed in north-east Queensland and are always fresh, not frozen. The photograph shows an informal arrangement of the ingredients, but if you want to serve it the way I like to at Bistro vue, follow the instructions in the method.

24 small–medium green Crystal Bay prawns
   (shrimp), peeled
1 baby fennel
10 peppercorns
1 lemon
1 large ripe avocado
Juice of ½ lemon
2 shallots, finely diced
5 drops Tabasco
1 cos lettuce
3 firm tomatoes, peeled and diced (see page 18)
2 tablespoons olive oil
½ bunch chives, chopped

MARY ROSE SAUCE
300 ml (10 fl oz) Mayonnaise (see page 14)
100 ml (3½ fl oz) tomato ketchup
Tabasco sauce
Salt and pepper

1 Devein the prawns by using a toothpick through the back of the prawn and lifting the prawn upwards.

2 Put 3 litres (6 pints) of water into a large heavy-based saucepan, add the fennel, peppercorns and whole lemon and bring to the boil. Have a bowl with lots of ice and cold water to the side. Add the prawns and cook for 1 minute. Remove and drop straight into the iced water. Set aside the pan of cooking liquid.

3 Make the Mary Rose sauce. Whisk the tomato ketchup into the mayonnaise, then whisk in Tabasco and salt and pepper to taste. Set aside.

4 Split the avocado in half, remove the stone and scoop out the flesh. Put into a food processor and blitz until smooth. Add the lemon juice, shallots and Tabasco and season to taste. Place in a bowl and cover tightly with cling film, to avoid discolouration. Reserve in the refrigerator.

5 Prepare the lettuce by removing and discarding the large outer leaves. Wash the inner leaves well and leave to dry on absorbent paper, then tear into large squares.

6 Dress the diced tomato with a little olive oil and the chopped chives.

7 Place a 10 cm (4 in) diameter pastry cutter on to a plate. Into this spoon a good tablespoon of the avocado purée and smooth it out on the plate to the edges of the cutter. Place 5–6 lettuce squares on top of the avocado followed by a large dollop of the Mary Rose sauce. Arrange 6 prawns on top and spoon a quarter of the tomato mix over them. Remove the pastry cutter and repeat the presentation on the other plates. Serve immediately.

ROAST SCALLOPS WITH CABBAGE SAUCE

SERVES 4

The method below for pan-frying the scallops will result in scallops that are still opaque in the centre, as my pet hate is overcooked scallops. Ensure the pan is properly hot before adding the scallops. I recommend using fresh scallops where possible but make sure they are large. The next-best option is frozen Canadian scallops which come in several sizes and are available worldwide in 1 kilogram (2 lb 3 oz) bags.

4 large outer green cabbage leaves
3 tablespoons finely sliced ginger
3 tablespoons olive oil
1 tablespoon thinly sliced garlic
3 tablespoons thinly sliced spring onions,
    white part only
250 ml (8½ fl oz) Chinese cooking wine
400 ml (13 fl oz) Chicken Stock (see page 17),
    heated until volume has reduced by half
2 tablespoons oyster sauce
2 tablespoons light mushroom soy sauce
12–16 large scallops, roe removed
1 tablespoon thyme sprigs
Lemon juice

1 Bring 2 litres (4 pints) of water to the boil over a high heat and put the cabbage leaves in the boiling water for 5 minutes or until tender. Add the ginger to the same water for 1 minute; remove both the ginger and cabbage; set aside on some absorbent paper.

2 Put 1 tablespoon of the olive oil in a saucepan over a medium heat. Add the ginger and fry (you need to hear the ginger sizzling) for 1 minute. The ginger should have no colour.

3 Add sliced garlic and fry for 30 seconds. Add the spring onions and fry for 30 seconds. Add the Chinese wine and reduce volume by two-thirds. Add the chicken stock, bring to the boil, and whisk in the oyster and mushroom soy sauces.

4 Add the cabbage, then put the sauce in a food processor or blender and purée for 5 minutes or until completely smooth. Pour the sauce equally over 4 warm plates.

5 Preheat a large frying pan over medium heat. Add the remaining olive oil, then add the scallops and thyme. Cook for 90 seconds or until the scallops are golden and turn over, cook for a further 30 seconds. Season the scallops with a squeeze of lemon juice.

6 Place 3–4 scallops on each plate, garnish with thyme and serve.

use fresh scallops:
Hervey Bay in Queensland
or Spring Bay in Tasmania
are good sources.

OYSTERS THE CLASSIC WAY

SERVES 4

Oysters have still got a long way to go in Australia in terms of quality. The only way to improve this is through knowledge and striving for better. Restaurant managers and chefs should never order oysters open, although it can be difficult to open them at home if you are inexperienced. Look for native varieties such as the Sydney rock and Angasi oysters. Moonlight Flat Oysters from Bateman's Bay in southern New South Wales is Australia's leading pioneer of proper farming practices in oyster production — look out for them.

12 merguez sausages
1 tablespoon olive oil
12 angasi oysters
Finely chopped shallots
12 lemon wedges
Freshly ground black pepper
12 slices of brown or rye bread

1 Heat a heavy-based skillet or pan over medium heat. Add the sausages and olive oil. Cook slowly until the sausages are golden and crisp.

2 Open the oysters with the correct knife and place 3 oysters on each plate. Place a pinch of shallot on each oyster followed by a squeeze of lemon juice and a twist of pepper from the mill.

3 Place the sausages, lemon wedges and brown bread on each plate and serve with a compulsory glass of crisp village Chablis.

BABA GHANOUSH

Most Middle Eastern and some Asian countries have a traditional eggplant dish, normally grilled, the flesh flavoured with onions and lemon juice and finished with olive oil. I particularly like the following recipe, which was given to me by my great mate Raymond Capaldi. It is a version that is derived traditionally from Egypt and is known as *mutabbal* in the Levant. If you add mayonnaise to the baba ghanoush it makes a sauce that can be served with grilled fish, while if you thin the dip with a little vegetable stock it becomes a delectable sauce over barbecued lamb.

2 eggplants
100 ml (3½ fl oz) tahini
150 ml (5 fl oz) Mayonnaise (see page 14)
Juice of 1 lemon
Salt and pepper
Pinch of ground cumin (optional)

1   Using a chargrill or barbecue, roast the eggplants on all sides until the skin becomes black. The eggplant will lose its shape and there will be a lot of water loss.

2   When the eggplants are cooked and soft, remove from the heat and drain in a colander. Allow to cool, then peel the skin and remove the stalk; discard both.

3   Put the flesh back into the colander, pressing out excess moisture. Transfer the eggplant to a liquidiser or food processor, blend on full power until smooth; slowly add the tahini and the mayonnaise whilst blending.

4   Season with lemon juice, salt and pepper, and cumin if desired. Serve in individual pots with toast or Sesame Salted French Toast (see page 21), or garnished with a handful of rocket drizzled with extra-virgin olive oil.

Most Middle Eastern and some Asian countries have a traditional eggplant dish.

CRISPY ASPARAGUS WITH BUTTER SAUCE

SERVES 4

This recipe may be used for either white or green asparagus. 'Crispy' asparagus may sound unusual but it is a very simple way of making the vegetable interesting and appealing to children. Choose very thick spears, no thinner than the diameter of an adult finger.

16 white asparagus spears
16 squares of 4 x 4 cm (2 x 2 in) aluminium foil
50 g (2 oz) plain (all-purpose) flour
2 eggs, beaten
200 g (7 oz) fine panko breadcrumbs
1 tablespoon olive oil
1 tablespoon cultured butter
1 tablespoon Murray River salt
Juice of ½ lemon

BUTTER SAUCE
500 ml (1 pint) Chicken Stock (see page 17)
1 tablespoon crushed garlic
Salt and freshly ground pepper
200 g (7 oz) cultured butter, diced

1 First make the sauce. In a heavy-based saucepan, reduce the chicken stock, garlic and seasoning until it is a quarter of the original volume. While it is still hot, remove the pan from the heat and whisk in the diced butter, a piece at a time, until sauce is thick and glossy. Set aside in a warm place.

2 Prepare the asparagus by holding each spear, one by one, at both ends and bending in the centre until it breaks in half. Discard the bottom end. Using a peeler, remove the outer skin of the asparagus and some of the spurs around the head.

3 Bring 4 litres (8 pints) of water to the boil over high heat. Blanch the spears in the boiling water for a minute then plunge them into ice-cold water; drain after 2 minutes.

4 Wrap a square of foil around the tip of each asparagus spear. Coat the spears in flour then dip into the beaten egg, then into breadcrumbs.

5 Heat a large, heavy-based frying pan over a medium heat. Add the olive oil and butter, then the asparagus and cook until golden, turning frequently by shaking the pan gently. Season with salt and lemon juice to taste.

6 Drain the golden asparagus on absorbent paper and remove the foil. Arrange 4 spears per plate and spoon the warm butter sauce over and around, or put sauce in a pot beside the spears for dipping.

BRAISED ARTICHOKES

Globe artichokes from the Provence have inspired chefs all over the world to conjure up ways to make this wonderful vegetable speak. I was taught the classic technique of cooking them in a very acidic blanc liquid, but it really overpowers the delicateness of the choke; I have found that cooking artichokes in a white meaty stock with as little acid as possible – but enough to stop them turning black – is the best way. My basic preparation now combines white wine and butter with artichokes and chicken stock. This dish is wonderful as a meal in itself or as an accompaniment to such delights as roast chicken or sea bass.

2 tablespoons virgin olive oil
10 small globe artichokes, peeled, base and
　leaves trimmed
1 large brown onion, thinly sliced
3 garlic cloves, thinly sliced
1 teaspoon sea salt
250 ml (8½ fl oz) white wine
500 ml (1 pint) Chicken Stock (see page 17)
2 tablespoons cultured butter

1　Heat the oil in a heavy-based saucepan over medium heat. Add the artichokes, onion, garlic, and a pinch of sea salt, then add the white wine. Cook for 5 minutes over a low heat with the lid tightly on. Add the chicken stock and butter and bring to the boil.

2　Reduce the heat to low and simmer for 20 minutes or until the artichokes are cooked. Slide a small knife into the heart of an artichoke: if the knife slides in with little force or pressure applied, then the artichoke is cooked.

3　Serve hot or cold; if cold, store everything in an airtight container overnight to allow the flavour to permeate through the artichokes.

Soups

Putting strong hoppy beer in
French Onion Soup adds an extra
dimension to its flavour.

FRENCH ONION SOUP

SERVES 6

I have included two serving suggestions here as I love this recipe so much. It can be served either as a simple lunch or as a feature on an extravagant dinner party menu by adding puff pastry to seal the soup bowl, which is then garnished with an ornate puff pastry lattice. Another great variation is to add beer or cider to the soup just before it is ready: approximately 100 ml (3½ fl oz) of alcohol per 300 ml (10 fl oz) serve, then simmer for a further minute to evaporate the alcohol before serving. The beer or wine adds an extra dimension to the soup's flavour.

50 ml (2 fl oz) duck fat
8 onions, evenly sliced
2 heads of garlic, finely chopped
500 ml (1 pint) white wine
2 litres (4 pints) Veal Stock (see page 16)
6 sprigs of thyme

TRADITIONAL TOPPING
12 large bread slices from a stale baguette
6 tablespoons grated gruyère cheese

PUFF PASTRY VARIATION
12 squares of puff pastry, about 5 mm (¼ in)
   thick and 2 cm (¾ in) diameter larger than the
   serving bowls
2 eggs, beaten
6 tablespoons grated gruyère cheese

1   In a heavy-based pan over low heat, melt the duck fat. Add the onions and cook slowly to caramelise. Add the garlic and cook for a further 2 minutes.

2   Deglaze the pan with the white wine. Add the veal stock and the thyme. Cook the liquid until it is reduced by one-third, then remove from the heat.

TRADITIONAL TOPPING

Preheat grill and toast baguette slices until golden on one side. Turn over, sprinkle the grated cheese over the croutons, and grill for 2 minutes or until cheese has melted and started to slightly colour. Serve soup in individual bowls, with a crouton on top.

PUFF PASTRY VARIATION

1   Prepare soup as above. Put soup in individual serving bowls and leave to chill in the refrigerator.

2   Measure the puff pastry to fit over the bowls with an excess of at least 2 cm (¾ in) around the edges. Put a piece of puff pastry over each bowl and seal the edges firmly. Brush the pastry top with egg wash then sprinkle grated cheese evenly over the top.

3   Using a lattice cutter, cut each remaining square of pastry and spread the lattice over the top of the egg-washed pastry, then gently seal the lattice edges over the top of the first layer. Rest pastry-topped bowls in the refrigerator for at least 30 minutes prior to baking.

4   Preheat oven to 180°C (350°F). Transfer bowls to oven and cook for 20 minutes, then turn the heat down to 120°C (250°F) for a further 10 minutes, to ensure the soup is heated through.

PUMPKIN AND PRAWN SOUP

SERVES 4

I learnt to make this recipe in a three-star establishment where the only ingredient not used in the recipe below was a tablespoon of crème fraiche whisked in before serving. I don't think it needs this final piece of finesse in the home environment. The soup freezes well, but remember to strain the herbs out before freezing. If prawns are not available then mussels are a fine substitute.

20 small green prawns (shrimp) (preferably Crystal Bay or school prawn)

3 tablespoons goose fat

1 brown onion, finely diced

250 ml (8½ fl oz) brandy

750 g (1 lb 10 oz) pumpkin, peeled and cut into 2–3 pieces

2 garlic cloves, crushed

1 litre (2 pints) sparkling mineral water

1 teaspoon sea salt

1 tablespoon chopped marjoram

1 tablespoon chopped parsley

1 Remove the prawn heads and shells and set aside. Put peeled prawns in the refrigerator.

2 Preheat a heavy-based pan about 40 cm (16 in) diameter over a medium flame. Add the goose fat and onion, sweat the onion until it becomes translucent, add the prawn heads and shells and stir for 5 minutes.

3 Turn heat up to high, add brandy and flambé it by turning the pan on an angle towards the flame (always tilt the pan away from your body). Add the pumpkin and garlic, stir and place the lid on the pan for a further 5 minutes over low heat. Remove the lid and check that the pumpkin has started to break down. Add the mineral water and salt.

4 Simmer for 20 minutes with the lid on until the pumpkin is soft. Preheat oven to 150°C (300°F).

5 Use a hand blender to purée the soup. If cooked correctly the pumpkin should have a silky smooth texture. Pass the soup through a mouli or coarse colander then strain once more, this time passing through a fine chinois or strainer. Put soup into a clean saucepan and bring to the boil over a high heat, adjust the salt and add the herbs.

6 Warm ovenproof serving bowls in the oven for a few minutes.

7 Place 5 peeled prawns in the bottom of each warm bowl and pour the boiling soup over the prawns. Serve immediately.

AVOCADO SOUP WITH SMOKED SALMON RILLETTES SERVES 4

Avocado is an item many chefs feature on their menus in salads but I have very rarely seen it served as a thick soup. I have not experimented with over-ripe avocados because I always try to buy avocados that are just right – by 'just right' I mean not too soft and not too firm. They have to have a little give in them but not so much that if force is applied your finger will break the skin. Verjus, for anyone who does not know, is unfermented grape juice and should have a touch of natural fructose — fruit sugar — which offsets the lime juice. Enjoy this dish as it is a real feel-good soup. I have found Viognier to be a great match with the herbaceous and acidic flavours of this recipe.

RILLETTES
8 slices smoked salmon (about 300 g/10 oz)
2 shallots, finely diced
100 g (3½ oz) celeriac, peeled and fine julienned
1 tablespoon fromage blanc (goat's cheese is fine)
1 tablespoon lilliput capers
1 lemon, zested and juiced
Sea salt to taste

SOUP
4 avocados, deseeded and peeled
Juice of 2 limes
250 ml (8½ fl oz) verjus
50 ml (2 fl oz) olive oil
Sea salt to taste
½ red onion, finely diced
1 tablespoon finely chopped chives
80 g (3 oz) caviar or salmon roe (optional)

1 Flake 4 slices of the smoked salmon and place in a mixing bowl along with the shallots and julienned celeriac.

2 Combine the other slices of smoked salmon, fromage blanc, lilliput capers, lemon zest and 1 teaspoon of lemon juice in a food processor. Purée for 1–2 minutes, until the mixture is relatively smooth.

3 Fold the purée into the flaked salmon and shallot mixture. Taste and adjust seasoning accordingly with remaining lemon juice and sea salt. Put in the refrigerator in a covered container to rest for 1 hour before serving.

4 To make the soup, put avocados, lime juice, verjus and olive oil into a blender and purée until smooth. Taste and season with sea salt accordingly. Pour into a bowl or jug and stir in the red onion and chives.

5 To serve, pour the soup equally into 4 chilled bowls, then using either an ice-cream scoop or spoon place a spoon of rillettes in each bowl. If budget allows, add 20 g (¾ oz) of either caviar or salmon roe on top of each spoonful of rillettes.

6 Serve whilst still chilled.

ALMOND GAZPACHO

SERVES 4

If anybody reading this recipe is partial to sea urchin but lacks an inspiration for serving it, I suggest that this white almond gazpacho is a very quick and easy accompaniment. The origins of gazpacho, in particular almond gazpacho, come from central Spain but you will find many similar versions of this classic chilled soup in the Basque region, where mostly they will contain cream, which I am not a huge fan of. When making gazpacho always rest the soup for at least 6 hours to release the potency of the onions and garlic – this will result in a much smoother taste.

200 g (7 oz) fresh shelled almonds or ground almonds
50 g (2 oz) fresh white sourdough bread, crusts removed, soaked in water
1 garlic clove, peeled
1 white onion, diced
300 g (10½ oz) sultana grapes, washed and picked
50 ml (2 fl oz) sherry vinegar
100 ml (3½ fl oz) extra-virgin olive oil, plus extra for serving
Sea salt

1 Put the almonds, sourdough, garlic, onion and grapes into a large bowl and use either a bar blender or a hand-held blender to purée all the ingredients together. Once smooth, leave the blender on the lowest power, add half the vinegar and slowly drizzle in the oil. Taste and adjust seasoning with remaining vinegar and salt.

2 Place in the refrigerator and rest for 6 hours before serving.

3 Serve with barbecued seafood (such as sea urchin) and garnish with a drizzle of extra-virgin olive oil.

Gazpacho comes from central Spain, but you will find many similar versions of this classic chilled soup in the Basque region.

I consider it a prerequisite to serve
a glass of New World Gewurztraminer
alongside this bowl of soup — French
cuisine at its most accessible.

FIFTEEN-MINUTE CRAYFISH NAGE

SERVES 2

This recipe works just as well with prawns, oysters, Moreton bay bugs and other shellfish, such as mussels. If food was ever meant to be served with wine this would be one of the dishes named in the top ten!

50 ml (2 fl oz) extra-virgin olive oil
1 x 800 g (1 lb 12 oz) crayfish (rock lobster),
   cooked and shelled, tail cut into medallions
Sea salt
500 g (1 lb 2 oz) clams
1 brown onion, finely diced
2 garlic cloves, crushed
6 baby carrots, peeled
1 leek, white part only, finely sliced
500 ml (1 pint) white wine
Juice of ½ lemon
Pepper
100 g (3½ oz) cultured butter
2 tablespoons basil leaves
1 tablespoon finely chopped tarragon
8 tablespoons cooked macaroni (made from
   4 tablespoons uncooked)

1 Preheat a large pot over medium heat, add the olive oil. Once the oil is hot, add the crayfish medallions and sauté for 1 minute, then season with sea salt.

2 Add the clams, followed by all the vegetables in quick succession. Sauté on high heat, stirring constantly.

3 Add the white wine and place the lid on the pot. Cook on high for 4 minutes.

4 Season with the lemon juice and salt and pepper. Add the butter, and stir well.

5 Once the butter is mixed into the bubbling juices, add the herbs and pasta, cook for 1 minute and serve.

CHICKEN, ZUCCHINI AND VEGETABLE BROTH WITH MINT

SERVES 4–6

The chicken wings can be replaced by any other flavour, such as roast lamb bones or prawn shells. I recommend not changing the chicken stock base as this is the foundation of the soup.

1 litre (2 pints) Chicken Stock (page 17)
5 chicken wings
1 small celeriac, finely diced
1 large potato, finely diced
½ brown onion
2 sprigs of thyme
1 large carrot, finely diced
½ celery stalk, finely diced
½ large leek, white part only, finely diced
1 large zucchini, finely diced
Salt and pepper
½ bunch of mint, leaves picked

1 Put the chicken wings and the stock in a large saucepan. Bring to a boil and gently simmer for 2 hours, skimming any fat from the surface.

2 Remove the wings from the stock, place on a tray and allow to cool. Pick the meat from the bones, discard the bones and shred the meat back into the stock.

3 Bring the stock back to the boil, add the celeriac, potato, onion and thyme and cook for 3–4 minutes. Add the carrot, celery and leek and cook for a further 4 minutes. Add the zucchini and cook for another minute.

4 Season well and remove from the heat. Rip the mint leaves into the broth, stir together and serve.

A simple soup for one of those lazy nights when you need something wholesome and have fresh bread on hand.

Light lunches & snacks

DUCK JAFFLE

SERVES 4

This recipe reminds me of when Dad would cook on a Sunday night and serve up bacon and eggs whether you wanted it or not – come to think of it, that was one of the main reasons I started cooking. Jaffles were my first attempt at creating my own meal out of necessity, which led the following week to homemade pizza. The photograph shows the dish cooked in a jaffle iron, but if you don't have one, follow the method below for cooking in a frying pan.

1 Confit Duck Leg, sliced (see page 22)
3 tablespoons goose fat
1 tablespoon finely chopped shallots
1 tablespoon finely chopped garlic
100 g (3½ oz) cooked White Beans (see page 24)
50 g (2 oz) diced tomato (see page 18)
1 tablespoon Tomato Fondue (see page 18)
150 ml (5 fl oz) Brown Chicken Stock (see page 17)
Salt and pepper
1 tablespoon finely chopped tarragon
1 tablespoon finely chopped parsley
8 slices sourdough bread
Butter

1 Place the slices of confit duck leg in a hot pan with the goose fat. When the meat is nicely caramelised, add chopped shallots and garlic. Then add the cooked white beans, diced tomato and tomato fondue and quickly sauté.

2 Add the chicken stock and simmer until liquid has evaporated. Season with salt and pepper and finish with chopped tarragon and parsley.

3 Preheat a frying pan over medium heat.

4 Brush one side of each piece of sourdough bread with butter and lay butter side down in the pan. Spread the cassoulet mix onto the sourdough, spreading to the edge, place another slice of sourdough on top with the butter side up. Cook on each side for 2 minutes or until golden brown.

5 Remove from the pan, cut in half on a diagonal and serve.

This recipe is perfect when you
have leftover confit duck legs, so it's
great for lunch the day following
a dinner party!

VEAL SKEWERS WITH DEEP-FRIED TUNA MAYONNAISE SERVES 4

I am the first to admit that this is one of the more difficult dishes to prepare in the book. Simply put, it is not simple – but hear me out. The dish looks and tastes decadent, but is very cost effective. It is also a great recipe to experiment with wine matches and I have found five that pair with it very well: Champagne, Riesling, Chardonnay, Gamay and Pinot Noir. Observe the photograph carefully, as presentation makes it all worthwhile. The tuna mayonnaise should be made in advance and kept in the freezer.

250 g (9 oz) piece of veal rump
Salt and pepper
Zest of 1 lemon
4 heaped tablespoons finely chopped parsley
4 heaped tablespoons finely chopped chives
1 tablespoon capers
1 anchovy, finely chopped
½ garlic clove, finely chopped
8 long rosemary sprigs

DEEP-FRIED TUNA MAYONNAISE
1 quantity Tuna Mayonnaise (see page 16)
100 g (3½ oz) plain (all purpose) flour
4 eggs, beaten
170 g (6 oz) panko breadcrumbs

1   With a sharp boning knife, remove all sinew and excess fat from the veal. Season it well.

2   Mix zest, herbs, capers, anchovy and garlic in a bowl and season mixture. Roll the veal in it and pat to cover thoroughly. Now roll veal up tightly in cling film, twisting the ends to create a firm 'sausage'. Knot the ends.

3   Bring 1 litre of water to the boil in a pan. Reduce to a simmer and add the veal; cover pan. Cook for 6 minutes then remove meat and leave to cool. Remove cling film and cut into 3 mm (¼ in) thick slices, 4 per portion.

DEEP-FRIED MAYONNAISE

1   Take mayonnaise out of the freezer. Using a hot knife, cut it into 2 cm (¾ in) cubes and return to the freezer. Take out a few cubes at a time, roll them in the flour, beaten egg (shake off excess) then breadcrumbs. Return to freezer until required.

2   Heat a heavy-bottomed frying pan and add a good quantity of oil. Add mayonnaise cubes in small batches and fry until golden. Drain on absorbent paper.

TO SERVE

1   Prepare skewers: remove the lower leaves from rosemary sprigs and using a sharp knife scrape away the bark. Fold a veal slice in half and thread on a skewer. Now add a mayonnaise cube. Repeat.

2   Serve two skewers per portion, ideally on the centre of a round wooden board, presented on a heavy cream plate.

QUAIL SCOTCH EGGS

SERVES 4

Scotch eggs are believed to have been invented by the food shop Fortnum & Mason in 1738 and so, contrary to popular belief, it is not a national dish of Scotland. Scotch eggs are commonly eaten cold, typically with salads and pickles, although they can be eaten hot. Quail eggs are found in all good Asian grocery shops; if they are not available then pigeon eggs are fine.

12 quail eggs
2 teaspoons white vinegar
2 tablespoons plain (all-purpose) flour
2 eggs, beaten
100 g (3½ oz) fine white breadcrumbs
1 litre (2 pints) vegetable oil

PORK MINCE MIX
500 g (1 lb 2 oz) pork mince
1 egg
1 tablespoon finely chopped parsley
1 tablespoon finely chopped chives
1 tablespoon finely chopped tarragon
1 tablespoon finally chopped shallots
1 teaspoon Dijon mustard
1 tablespoon goose fat
Salt and pepper

1 Cook eggs in boiling water for 3 minutes. Immediately put them into iced water so they don't overcook (the yolks should still be runny).

2 Add white vinegar to the iced water. A chemical reaction will take place over the next 10 minutes that makes the shells soft and easy to peel. Peel the shells and remove the inner membrane, then wash eggs to make sure all remains of these are removed. Set aside until required.

3 To make the pork coating, combine all ingredients in a food processor and blend until they have been incorporated. Using a large ice-cream scoop, make 12 portions of the mince, then using your thumb press into the middle of each ball to create a cavity that an egg will fit into. Place an egg in each cavity and close up by using your fingers to pinch the gap.

4 Dip each ball lightly into the flour then into the beaten egg, and roll in the breadcrumbs; refrigerate balls until required.

5 Before serving, put the vegetable oil in a large heavy-based saucepan and bring to 180°C (350°F) using a thermometer. Place 2 eggs into the oil at a time and cook for 3–4 minutes or until golden. Repeat cooking for all eggs. Let the eggs rest for 10 minutes before cutting in half to ensure they are cooked. If they are not sufficiently cooked place them in a warm oven at 160°C (320°F) for 5 minutes.

6 Serve with your favourite tomato chutney or relish.

Using quail eggs rather than hen's eggs is a great option for home as they are a better size and offer something different and slightly exotic.

MOULES FRITES

This recipe has the same flavours as a soup I ate at Marco Pierre White's The Restaurant in the late 1990s in London's very swish Knightsbridge, where I later became an employee, but the method is simpler and the time involved is a lot less! It is a dish that will make a great entrée or light main course. The key technique to grasp here is the cooking of the mussels; apply this method to all shellfish. Serve the mussels with some great sourdough bread and good butter, French fries and homemade mayonnaise. Big, fat and plump, good-quality mussels should not need soaking in cold water to remove excess sand and grit – gritty mussels are usually a sign that the mussels have been dredged. Simply wash the fresh mussels under cold running water and remove the beard by pulling it away from the shell before cooking.

2 kg (4 lb 8 oz) large Tasmanian Spring
   Bay mussels
5 shallots
2 garlic cloves
100 ml (3½ fl oz) olive oil
3 sprigs of fresh thyme
500 ml (1 pint) white wine
4 portions of crisp French Fries (see page 155)
4 tablespoons Mayonnaise (see page 14)

1 Wash mussels under cold running water and remove the beards. Peel and slice shallots and garlic.

2 Choose a large, heavy-based pan with a lid. Heat on medium-high heat, add olive oil, shallots, garlic and thyme and cook very briefly. Add the mussels and white wine and cover with the lid.

3 Let the mussels steam in their own juices for approximately 5 minutes or until the shells have opened. The mussels should be plump, well open and shiny in appearance.

4 Remove the mussels from the pot into a colander with a suitable container underneath to catch the juices. Discard any mussels that have not opened.

5 Divide the mussels and cooking liquid between 4 hot bowls. Serve with the French fries and mayonnaise.

CRAB RILLETTES
WITH PINK GRAPEFRUIT AND GLOBE ARTICHOKES   SERVES 8

A classic dish that is so French and so easy to produce at home you will wonder why there is such a thing as a chef. Well, almost … Brown crabmeat is not difficult to obtain: it is the flesh found in the head. Its texture will vary with the variety of crab but it has an amazing crabby flavour and is used widely by Europeans to flavour soups and sauces. It is not dissimilar to the coral found in the head of a lobster. Your fishmonger will be able to help you to obtain it.

2 leaves of titanium gelatine
100 ml (3½ fl oz) cognac
100 ml (3½ fl oz) Seafood Stock (see page 120)
2 garlic cloves, crushed
1 tablespoon finely chopped tarragon
100 g (3½ oz) brown crabmeat
500 g (1 lb 2 oz) white crabmeat
Juice of 1 lemon
Salt and freshly ground black pepper
350 ml (12 fl oz) semi-whipped cream
8 Braised Artichokes (see page 44)
2 ruby grapefruit, peeled and segmented

1 Soak the gelatine in cold water for 10 minutes. Squeeze out excess water.

2 Pour the cognac into a heavy-based saucepan, flambé carefully and reduce by half. Add the stock, garlic and tarragon and cook until volume has again reduced by half.

3 Gently warm the brown crabmeat in a separate heavy-based saucepan. Add the gelatine, stir it through carefully, transfer to a mixing bowl and fold in the white crabmeat. Add the lemon juice, season with salt and pepper then fold in the cream.

4 Spoon the mixture into a greased deep tray or ceramic bowl. Transfer to the refrigerator for 24 hours.

5 Put an artichoke in the centre of each serving plate. Using two dessertspoons, form quenelles (oval shapes) of crab rillettes and place one in each artichoke.

6 Arrange grapefruit segments on the plate. Serve with dressed seasonal salad leaves and Melba toast or brioche.

This traditional open pie is topped with a scattering of black olives and anchovies ... but variations have crept into the original recipe.

PISSALADIERE

This Provençale version of pizza has its origins in Nice. I had a lot of trouble finding out why it has such a strange name but Elizabeth David's *French Provincial Cooking* gave me t o the original recipe and I see this as a benefit. This recipe is made with simple crisp puff pastry – the traditional base was a potato and flour dough – but for a simpler alternative place the toppings on toasted baguette. The onion jam can be made well in advance.

3 brown onions
100 ml (3½ fl oz) duck fat
2 sprigs of thyme
1 red capsicum (bell pepper)
4 x 10 cm (4 in) diameter circles of puff pastry
About 50 pitted kalamata olives
5 Ortiz anchovies or 15–20 smaller anchovies
20 g (¾ oz) thick Tomato Fondue (see page 18)

1 Peel and thickly slice the onions. In a heavy-based pan over medium heat, heat the duck fat and gently fry the onions. Add the thyme. Stir often until the onion has caramelised (in the same way as for French onion soup). Remove pan from the heat and set aside.

2 Over a flame, char the capsicum until the skin has blackened. Put in a small bowl and cover with cling film (this will help the skin come off more easily). Once the capsicum is cool enough to handle, remove the top and bottom, split lengthways and discard the seeds and white membrane. Peel off the blackened skin and discard. Using a sharp knife, cut the flesh into thin strips and set aside.

3 Preheat the oven to 170°C (340°F).

4 Using a fork, gently stab the surface of the puff pastry discs to create small holes. Line a tray with baking paper, place the pastry on top of the paper. Put another layer of baking paper over the discs and then place another baking tray on top of the discs (so they don't rise when cooking). Bake in the oven for 15 minutes or until golden.

5 Cut the olives in half. Cut the anchovies into strips the same size as the capsicum.

6 To assemble, place a pastry cutter about 1 cm (½ in) smaller in diameter than the puff pastry circle on top of the pastry. Spread a thin layer of tomato fondue into the cutter (that is, on to the pastry) then a thin layer of the caramelised onions on top of this. Remove the pastry cutter and criss-cross the top with 5 strips of capsicum and 5 strips of anchovy; place olive cheeks round side up in the gaps between the strips and serve.

MUSHROOM RISOTTO

SERVES 4 AS A LIGHT MAIN COURSE

Be patient when making risotto, and have a small amount of hot stock reserved to fold through it when it is time to serve. The Champagne vinegar in this recipe lifts the flavour of the rice and balances the richness of the butter. A New World Pinot Gris with a little age cuts through the richness of this dish and can have a 'mushroomy' flavour itself. This recipe will take no longer than 25 minutes to assemble and serve. The extravagant cook could grate some fresh truffle into the rice whilst cooking, then garnish with extra slices of truffle before serving.

2½ tablespoons olive oil
1 onion, finely diced
250 g (9 oz) carnaroli rice
350 ml (12 fl oz) dry white wine
500 ml (1 pint) Chicken Stock (see page 17)
300 ml (10 fl oz) Mushroom Stock (see page 24)
100 g (3½ oz) cultured butter, finely diced
2 tablespoons Champagne vinegar
60 g (2 oz) Grana Padano cheese, grated
½ tablespoon chopped tarragon
Salt and freshly ground pepper
1 quantity Mushroom Fricassee (see page 47)

1 Heat the olive oil in a heavy-based saucepan, add the onion and cook over low heat for 3 minutes or until soft but not coloured. Add the rice, stirring until each grain is coated with oil.

2 Meanwhile, bring the chicken stock to the boil in a heavy-based saucepan, then lower heat to keep warm.

3 Increase the heat under the rice to medium, add the wine and deglaze, stirring well. Cook until the wine has evaporated, stirring with a wooden spoon to prevent sticking. Add most of the chicken stock and cook, stirring occasionally, for 5 minutes or until the stock is absorbed.

4 In a small heavy-based saucepan, bring the mushroom stock to the boil, then reduce heat to low. Add enough hot mushroom stock to just cover the rice and simmer until the rice has absorbed all the liquid, occasionally stirring with a wooden spoon. Remove from the heat.

5 Add the butter, 1 tablespoon of the vinegar, a good pinch of cheese and the tarragon, and gently fold these through the rice. If the risotto appears a little firm, add the reserved chicken stock to loosen the texture. Add more vinegar to taste. Season with salt and pepper.

6 Warm the mushroom fricasse over low heat.

7 Divide risotto between serving plates and then spoon the mushroom fricassee over and around the rice. Serve immediately.

Organic free-range eggs
come into their own with
dishes like this.

EGGS COCOTTE WITH PEAS AND BACON

SERVES 4

Organic free-range eggs come into their own with dishes like this, the purity of the egg yolks can be seen as well as tasted. A good tip to tell whether eggs are fresh is that the egg white should be firm and not runny, and when the egg is broken it should sit approximately 2–3 mm ($^1/_8$ in) above the plate. As eggs get older the cells in the egg white naturally break down, causing the white to become runny.

Serve the eggs with toasted sourdough fingers that have been fried in a very small amount of olive oil and then rolled in crushed sesame seeds and sea salt. This little tip turns the dish from a simple brunch recipe into a dinner party winner. Truffle sliced very liberally over the top before serving makes this dish iconic.

1 tablespoon cultured butter
1 brown onion, finely diced
2 garlic cloves, crushed
4 tablespoons fresh peas, shelled
8 bacon rashers, cut into strips
Sea salt and pepper
4 tablespoons extra-virgin olive oil
8 eggs
8 slices rye sourdough bread
Butter, for toast
1 tablespoon finely chopped parsley

1 Preheat the oven to 140°C (275°F).

2 Heat a heavy-based frying pan over a low heat. Add butter, onions, garlic, peas and sweat for 3–4 minutes. Add the bacon and season well.

3 Place 4 cocotte dishes (capacity 250 ml/8½ fl oz) or ramekin moulds into a deep oven tray. Fill the tray with boiling water a third of the way up the sides of the dishes. Put 1 tablespoon of olive oil in the bottom of each dish, and top with the pea mixture, divided in equal quantities between each dish.

4 Break the eggs into a small bowl one at a time and add 2 eggs to each dish.

5 Cover the tray tightly with aluminium foil. Place in the oven for 20 minutes. The eggs are ready when they are soft but the whites should be cooked through.

6 Whilst the eggs are cooking, grill or toast the sourdough, spread with butter and season with sea salt and pepper.

7 Remove the tray from the oven, remove the foil and place each dish on a plate with 2 slices of toast, sprinkle generously with parsley and serve.

POTATO AND CAPER TERRINE

SERVES 4

Everybody loves potato salad and this idea is a simple way of turning a well-loved staple into a time-conscious dish that can be adapted and evolved as you become familiar with the recipe. An example of this is when I tested the recipe, I served it with a piece of grilled swordfish draped over the top of the potato.

8 medium-sized kipfler potatoes
4 tablespoons Mayonnaise (see page 14)
1 shallot, finely diced
4 tablespoons fine lilliput capers
2 Ortiz anchovies, crushed
4 tablespoons fried bacon or ham lardons
Sea salt and pepper
4 egg yolks
500 ml (1 pint) vegetable oil
2 handfuls curly endive
1 tablespoon olive oil

1 Put the kipfler potatoes into a pot of cold water, add 1 tablespoon of salt and bring to the boil. Cook until tender. Test the potatoes by inserting a small knife into a potato – it is important that they are well cooked.

2 Once cooked, drain and cool. When they are cool enough to touch, peel.

3 Place the potatoes in a mixing bowl, add the mayonnaise, shallot, capers, anchovies, bacon and salt and pepper, and mix well to crush the potatoes.

4 Arrange 4 plates on an organised work surface ready for serving.

5 Spoon the mixture into the centre of the plates using an 8 cm (3½ in) round ring or cutter to guide the shape. Press the mixture in well with the back of a spoon.

6 Put the vegetable oil into a flat-bottomed pot and warm over a low heat to approximately 60°C (140°F). Add the egg yolks carefully without breaking them, remove the pan from the heat and allow the yolks to warm through for 4 minutes. Carefully remove the yolks using a slotted spoon. Drain on absorbent paper.

7 Remove the rings from around the terrines, place an egg yolk on top of each, taking care not to break them.

8 Put the curly endive into a small bowl with the olive oil and toss together. Place the dressed endive over and around the plate. Season the egg with salt and pepper and serve immediately.

WELSH RAREBIT

The Welsh have been eating cheese on toast at least since the early 1700s, when the first documented recipe appeared. This fancy version can be used as a Sunday night special or manipulated into a canapé for a special occasion. I like it so much that since testing this recipe I have placed it on the Café Vue menu. Any hard cheese will do but cheddar or gruyère is preferable.

Good sourdough bread
40 g (1½ oz) unsalted butter
50 g (2 oz) plain (all purpose) flour
250 ml (8½ fl oz) cider
250 g (9 oz) Ironstone mature cheddar, grated
1 tablespoon Dijon mustard
1 teaspoon Worcestershire sauce
1 egg yolk
Salt and pepper, to taste
Additional 20 g (¾ oz) unsalted butter

1   Slice the bread to make 6 slices, about 2.5 cm (1 in) thick.

2   Melt the 40 g (1½ oz) butter in a heavy-based saucepan, add the flour and cook on low heat, gently stirring with a wooden spoon, until the flour and butter come together. Allow the roux to cook for a further minute.

3   Slowly add the cider, stirring, and cook over a medium heat for 2 minutes, to make a thick velouté.

4   Remove from the heat, add the grated cheese, whisk together until smooth. Add the mustard, Worcestershire sauce, whisk in the egg yolk and add salt and pepper to taste.

5   Leave to cool in the refrigerator for 3 hours.

6   Preheat the grill.

7   Lay the slices of bread evenly on a tray. Toast one side of the bread, and then butter the other side. Spread a very thick layer of cheese mixture on top and put under the grill again until golden.

8   Cut into triangles and serve.

Salads

NICOISE SALAD

Salad niçoise is the most famous of all salads, consisting of potatoes, tuna, olives, green beans and vinaigrette dressing. Its correct ingredients are often disputed, while even the way it is assembled can cause arguments. Some people say it should be served on a bed of lettuce while others say that tomatoes are the base. And some don't arrange the elements of the salad at all, but toss it all together. Use the photograph as a more elaborate guide to plating for a dinner party. 'Niçoise' is a term used for dishes served with ingredients used by the chefs of the city of Nice, in the south of France. They include garlic, tomatoes, anchovies, black olives, capers and lemon juice.

1 small baguette (1–2 days old preferably)
2 tablespoons extra-virgin olive oil
Salt and pepper
1 garlic clove, peeled
2 large eggs
20 green beans, trimmed and tailed
4 small tomatoes (fresh, semi-dried or confit)
4 small kipfler potatoes, boiled and sliced
   into discs
4 teaspoons lilliput capers
1 red onion, cut into 5 mm (¼ in) rings
50 g (2 oz) olives
200 ml (7 fl oz) olive oil
40 ml (1½ fl oz) sherry vinegar
4 x 100 g (3½ oz) fish fillets (tuna, red mullet
   or kingfish)
4 tablespoons baby rocket
1 lemon, halved

1 Preheat the oven to 180°C (350°F). Slice the baguette into 1 cm (½ in) thick slices and lay on a flat baking tray. Brush with olive oil and sprinkle with salt. Bake for 5–6 minutes, then remove from oven and rub slices with the garlic clove.

2 Put the eggs in a saucepan, cover with water and bring to the boil. Take out after 6 minutes, when the yolks will still be soft. Set aside and keep warm.

3 Place another pan on the stove, fill with 2 litres (5 pints) of salted water and bring to the boil. Add the beans and blanch for 2 minutes. Remove beans and refresh by placing in iced water for 2 minutes, until cold.

4 In a stainless steel bowl combine the croutons, tomatoes, beans, potatoes, capers, onion and olives, season well.

5 In a separate bowl or jar, mix the 200 ml olive oil and sherry vinegar well.

6 Preheat a non-stick pan over medium heat. Season the fish and brush with more olive oil. Reduce heat to low, place the fish skin side down in the pan and cook for 2–3 minutes. Turn fish over and cook for a further minute.

7 Toss the salad together with the dressing.

8 To serve, set out 4 flat bowls or plates and place a fillet in the centre of each. Arrange the salad neatly around the fish. Peel the eggs carefully, cut in half, season them and arrange on top of the salad. Scatter baby rocket over and serve with a wedge of lemon on the side.

SCALLOP AND WATERMELON SALAD

A very Australian dish, with a sense of simplicity. It combines two ingredients which might not necessarily work together if they were complicated by other ingredients. Presentation is very important with this dish, don't just mix it all up in a bowl and serve. You have to think Japanese, 'less is more', in terms of separating the flavours both with the eye and the palate. I would even go so far as thinking of drinking very cold sake with this dish – and an ocean view also helps! You need to prepare the watermelon jelly the day before you want to serve this salad.

1 kg (2 lb 3 oz) watermelon
6 leaves of titanium gelatine, soaked in cold water
8 scallops, cleaned and trimmed, roe removed
1 teaspoon garlic oil
2 teaspoons yuzu juice
Salt and pepper
Sunflower shoots

1 Remove the skin from the melon and cut into 1 cm (½ in) cubes. Put half of the cubes in the refrigerator. Put the other half in a food processor and purée until liquid. Pass through a fine sieve to remove any seeds and lumps.

2 Remove the softened gelatine from the water, drain well. Pour the watermelon liquid into a heavy-based saucepan over medium heat and bring to 60°C (140°F), then whisk in the gelatine until dissolved.

3 Pass watermelon liquid through a fine sieve. Pour into a deep tray, place in the refrigerator and allow to set overnight, for a minimum of 8 hours, or until firm.

4 Using a 1 cm (½ in) round metal cutter, cut tubes of jelly out of the tray. Slice the tubes into thin discs with a knife.

5 Slice each scallop into 3 or 4 slices depending on how thick the scallops are.

6 Place the scallop slices in a bowl with the garlic oil and yuzu juice and season well, toss together and allow to marinate for 10 minutes.

7 On each plate arrange 5 scallop slices randomly, then place 5 watermelon jelly discs and 5 watermelon cubes around the plate. Place a sunflower shoot on each watermelon cube and serve.

CAESAR SALAD

The original 'Caesar salad' recipe credits the creation of the dish to an Italian immigrant, Caesar Cardini, who operated a restaurant in Tijuana. According to the canonical version, told by Caesar's daughter Rosa, he tossed the first Caesar salad on the evening of 4 July 1924. It is said that on this busy weekend, Cardini was running low on food and he put together a salad for his guests from what was left over in the kitchen. The original salad did not contain anchovies as Worcestershire sauce at the time had a very pungent fishy odour, but this sauce evolved over time to suit consumer palates, reducing its fish content, so anchovies were added to the salad. For an additional flourish I like to add grilled prawns to the salad (see recipe for Marinated Prawns with Cauliflower Couscous, page 118).

2 bread rolls, preferably white
2 tablespoons light oil or clarified butter
Sea salt and pepper
8 tablespoons bacon lardons
3 standard cos lettuces, leaves picked and washed
8 tablespoons Grana Padano cheese shavings

DRESSING
4 egg yolks
1 tablespoon Dijon mustard
1 tablespoon creamed horseradish
6 anchovies, crushed
1 tablespoon white wine vinegar
100 g (3½ oz) Grana Padano cheese, grated
2 tablespoons Worcestershire sauce
Juice of ½ lemon
250 ml (8½ fl oz) vegetable oil

1   In a bowl combine all the ingredients for the dressing except the oil and only use half of the lemon juice; whisk together until completely combined.

2   Slowly drizzle the oil into the bowl, whisking constantly, until the dressing becomes thick. If the dressing becomes so thick that you feel it may split add some of the reserved lemon juice or a touch of water to loosen it.

3   Taste and adjust the balance of acid by adding a little of the remaining lemon juice, if necessary. Set aside.

4   Preheat oven to 160°C (320°F).

5   Slice the bread into 3 mm (¼ in) thick slices. Lay them on a flat tray and brush each with clarified butter or light oil. Season with salt and bake in oven for 5 minutes, or until golden, then remove from oven and allow to cool.

6   Gently fry bacon lardons in a frying pan until golden and crisp, then drain on aborbent paper.

7   Put toasted slices, lettuce leaves, bacon and cheese shavings into a large bowl. Add 8 tablespoons of dressing, season with salt and pepper, toss the salad until the dressing evenly coats the leaves. Serve in equal amounts.

DUCK SALAD

This is a recipe with several elements, but think of the old saying, 'the harder you work the luckier you get'. Whoever eats this dish will be a very lucky person, particularly when it is matched with an aromatic glass of Alsatian Pinot Gris.

4 Confit Duck Legs (see page 22)
1 bread roll, preferably white
2 tablespoons light oil or clarified butter
Sea salt
1 tablespoon duck fat
Salt and pepper
4 small eggs, 40–50 g (1½–2 oz) each, soft
    poached (see page 15)
1 pear (Williams' or Packham's are most suitable)
300 g (10 oz) frisee lettuce
24 walnut halves
2 shallots, finely diced
20 ml (1 fl oz) extra-virgin olive oil
50 ml (2 fl oz) sherry vinegar

CONFIT DUCK

Begin preparations to confit the duck legs 1–2 days in advance of the remainder of the salad (see page 22).

CROUTONS

1 Preheat oven to 160°C (32°F).

2 Slice the bread into 3 mm (¼ in) thick slices. Lay them on a flat tray and brush each with clarified butter or light oil. Season with sea salt and bake in oven for 5 minutes, or until golden.

TO PREPARE SALAD

1 Preheat a skillet or frying pan to a medium heat, add the duck fat. Season the confit duck legs with salt and pepper and add to the pan. Cook skin side down for 2–3 minutes, until crispy. Turn the legs over and briefly cook for 1–2 minutes skin side up.

2 Remove the duck legs from the pan, drain on absorbent paper and place each in the centre of a serving plate. Place a poached egg directly on the top of each duck leg.

3 Peel and julienne the pear into matchstick-sized sticks. Remove any yellow leaves from the frisee, wash green leaves thoroughly and pat dry. Place the pear and frisee leaves in a mixing bowl together with the walnuts, shallots and croutons.

4 In a separate bowl mix the olive oil and sherry vinegar together until emulsified, add a third of this to the salad and toss together, making sure all the leaves are thoroughly covered.

5 Add the salad to each plate by scattering it over and around the duck leg. Spoon the remaining dressing over and around and serve.

WALDORF SALAD

The classic salad is back in a big way as far as I'm concerned: I'm really enjoying serving retro salads as appetisers. I have researched the history of the dishes, so I can re-create them as they were designed to be served. Another way of presentation is to serve the salad on a piece of crispy baguette that has been baked in the oven for 5 minutes and then rubbed with a garlic clove; for more variation you can add crab meat or shredded chicken to the salad before serving. Waldorf salad is great accompanied by any light white or sparkling wine.

1 small celeriac
1 green apple
1 brown onion, finely diced
100 g (3½ oz) walnut halves
Juice of ½ lemon
2 tablespoons Mayonnaise (see page 14)
Sea salt and freshly ground black pepper
250 ml (8½ fl oz) vegetable oil
6 quail eggs

1 Peel the celeriac using a serrated knife in the same manner as you would an orange, starting by cutting off the top and bottom of the celeriac, then using a downward motion cut the rough outside skin away.

2 Slice the peeled celeriac into 3 mm (¼ in) slices, then julienne these into long thin strips.

3 Cut the apple in a similar manner, but there is no need to peel it, although you should remove the core.

4 Put the celeriac and apple in a metal mixing bowl along with the onion, walnuts, lemon juice, mayonnaise, a little salt and pepper. Toss together well and taste; season more if necessary and when the taste is agreeable, set the salad aside.

5 Preheat a non-stick pan over a low heat, add the vegetable oil. Gently break open the eggs and add to the pan. Keep the pan on a very low heat and cook for 2 minutes until the egg whites are just cooked.

6 Remove pan from the heat and allow the eggs to sit in the warm oil for a further 1–2 minutes, then slide the eggs onto a plate and, using a small round cutter, trim the whites neatly into circles.

7 Place a good amount of salad on the centre of each plate, top with a fried egg in the centre and serve.

ZUCCHINI SALAD
SERVES 4

Courgettes — or zucchini, as we know them here in Australia — are a very underrated vegetable. I rarely see them served except in overcooked ratatouille at functions, yet they are in every greengrocer and supermarket I visit. What happens to them? I hope this recipe gives you ideas other than letting them rot in the refrigerator and then throwing them away. In this salad the zucchini is served raw, making it especially nutritious. If you want to serve this salad as an entrée, simply add a little flair to the final dish by stuffing zucchini flowers (available from October to late April) with soft goat's cheese, dipping them in batter and frying at 180°C (350°F) until golden, then place one on top of each salad and serve.

4 large green zucchini, coarsely grated
2 tablespoons finely diced shallots
2 teaspoons finely chopped tarragon
Salt and pepper
1 tablespoon walnut oil
1 teaspoon sherry vinegar

1 Combine the grated zucchini and shallots in a bowl, then add the finely chopped tarragon. Season with salt and pepper.

2 In a separate bowl, combine the walnut oil and vinegar with a whisk or fork. Add to the zucchini and mix thoroughly with seasoning as required and serve.

WATERCRESS AND HAZELNUT SALAD

SERVES 6

Wash and prepare this salad as close as possible to serving time.

200 g (6½ oz) hazelnuts
6 cups watercress
5 shallots, finely chopped
Salt and freshly ground black pepper
2½ tablespoons French Vinaigrette (see page 14)

1 Preheat the oven to 180°C (350°F). Roast the hazelnuts in the oven for 5–8 minutes or until the skin easily rubs off between the fingers. Peel and coarsely crush.

2 Put the hazelnuts, watercress and shallots in a serving bowl, mix and season.

3 Dress the salad with the vinaigrette. Season and serve immediately.

TOMATO SALAD WITH BLACK OLIVE DRESSING

SERVES 4

This salad relies on using beautifully ripe, juicy tomatoes – which can be a challenge, especially during the winter months. Below are my recommendations for tomato varieties to look out for across the four seasons. If you are growing tomatoes at home they should be planted no later than September in the Southern Hemisphere for harvest in the following six months.

150 g (5 oz) kalamata olives, pitted
300 ml (10 fl oz) olive oil
8 Black Russian or good roma (plum) tomatoes
1 tablespoon finely chopped shallots
1 garlic clove, crushed
100 g (3½ oz) kalamata olives, pitted
1 punnet baby basil shoots
Sea salt and pepper

I   For the dressing, preheat the oven to 120°C (250°F). Put the 150 g (5 oz) pitted olives on a tray lined with baking paper and place in the oven for 4 hours. When the olives are dry and wrinkled remove from the oven and place in a food processor with the olive oil. Blitz until a smooth black oil is achieved – this may take up to 5 minutes.

2   Thinly slice the tomatoes, place in a bowl with the shallots and garlic and gently mix together. Arrange the tomatoes on a plate. Cut the remaining olives in half and scatter over the tomatoes. Sprinkle the baby basil shoots over the top.

3   Season the tomatoes generously with pepper and salt, drizzle the dressing over the salad.

SUMMER
Roma (plum)

AUTUMN
Zebra, Black Russian

WINTER
Adelaide

SPRING
Heirloom varieties such as
Brandywine and Big Rainbow

seafood

MARINATED KINGFISH WITH YUZU AND WATTLESEED

SERVES 4

This dish looks flamboyant and needs the cook to be in the mood for creative fare. The spice of ground wattleseed gives the subtle flesh of sea-flavoured kingfish a hit of acidity, followed by a slight aromatic bitterness. For an extra dimension, this dish can be combined with freshly diced watermelon for a clean finish on the palate and a dash of exciting colour.

500 g (1 lb 2 oz) hiramasa kingfish, trimmed
4 shallots, finely diced
2 garlic cloves, crushed
2 teaspoons yuzu juice
4 tablespoons extra-virgin olive oil
1 tablespoon oyster sauce
2 teaspoons finely sliced on the diagonal
   spring onions
Sea salt and pepper
1 teaspoon wattleseed, crushed

GARNISH (OPTIONAL)
Small baby herb shoots or sliced baby radishes or
   watermelon cubes

1 Slice the kingfish across the loin to create 1 cm (½ in) thick discs.

2 Place 4 even portions on each plate.

3 To make dressing, combine shallots, garlic, yuzu juice, olive oil and oyster sauce in a small bowl.

4 Pour the dressing liberally over the kingfish on each plate.

5 Sprinkle with the spring onions, season with sea salt and pepper.

6 Season with the wattleseed as you would with pepper.

7 Garnish the plates with small baby herb shoots or sliced baby radishes.

JOHN DORY A LA MEUNIERE

Undoubtedly 'à la meunière' is the hardest 'simple' technique there is. To cook a perfect piece of fish over a stove is all about knowing your stove and how to control the heat. The fish needs to be golden and crisp on the outside yet moist and barely cooked on the inside. Finish with golden nutty French butter, lemon and herbaceous parsley, then you have the perfect piece of nature on a plate – yet how many chefs, yet alone home cooks, know how to, or even want to, cook a beautiful piece of fish correctly?

4 John Dory fillets (200–300 g/7–10 oz each)
2 tablespoons olive oil
100 g (3½ oz) plain (all purpose) flour
300 g (10 oz) cultured butter
1 lemon, cut in half
1 tablespoon finely chopped parsley
Sea salt and freshly ground white pepper

1 Clean and trim the fillets, making sure all the bones are removed.

2 Heat a large heavy-based skillet or saucepan over a medium to high heat, then add the olive oil.

3 Dip each fillet into the flour. Pat lightly to remove excess flour.

4 Cook the fish fillets 2 at a time. Do not cram the pan with fish as it will lower the temperature and ruin the dish. Sauté fillets for 2 minutes on each side or until golden, remove from the pan and cook the remaining fillets. Then put all the fillets back into the pan.

5 Add the butter and let it bubble and froth before adding a squeeze of lemon juice and the parsley.

6 Season with salt and pepper.

7 Using a metal kitchen spoon, spoon the melted butter over the fillets to flavour the top side of the fish with the lovely nutty taste.

8 Place each fillet on a warmed serving plate and serve immediately.

Finish with golden nutty French
butter, lemon and herbaceous parsley,
then you have the perfect piece of
nature on a plate ...

Just remember to take care
when folding the bag and
don't crease or pierce the foil.

SNAPPER BAKED IN A BAG

Cooking in a bag is so logical: when I think about it for too long it becomes frustrating that I didn't think of it earlier in my career! Serving is easy and stress free, and the preparation is methodical and not reliant on creative flamboyance.

2 tablespoons extra-virgin olive oil
4 tablespoons diced celery
1 onion, diced
2 garlic cloves, crushed
4 tablespoons cultured butter
4 tablespoons blanched and shelled broad beans
Sea salt and pepper
4 x 150 g (5 oz) pieces of snapper, skin removed
Juice of 1 lime
Additional extra-virgin olive oil

TO MAKE FOIL BAGS

1 Take 8 sheets of aluminium foil approximately 30 cm (12 in) square. Take 2 sheets of foil and put the non-shiny sides together. Repeat with remaining squares.

2 Brush the top of each double square with olive oil, to prevent the fish sticking.

3 Fold three of the edges inwards several times to create a well-sealed pouch – the fourth side will be sealed once the ingredients have been placed inside.

TO COOK FISH

1 Preheat the oven to 200°C (400°F).

2 Put a heavy-based pan over a medium flame, add the olive oil, celery, onion and garlic, and sweat the vegetables for 2–3 minutes. Add the butter and whisk until smooth and shiny, then add the broad beans, mix together, season well and remove from heat.

3 Season the fish with salt and lime juice. Place a piece of the fish in each foil bag, followed by a spoonful of the broad bean mixture. Add another drizzle of olive oil before sealing each bag tightly.

4 Lay the bags flat on a rack resting on an oven tray. Place in the oven and cook for 20 minutes.

5 Remove from the oven, cut open the bag and remove the fish, vegetables and juices to a plate (be careful of the steam that will escape from the bag once open).

6 Serve with a celery leaf salad and crusty bread.

MARINATED TOMMY RUFF WITH CARROT VINAIGRETTE AND BROCCOLI COUSCOUS

SERVES 4

You may wonder what tommy ruff is. It is a fish you probably have seen a hundred times but have always ignored or overlooked. Tommy ruff is another name for Australian herring (*Arripis georgianus*), which are also called ruffies or sea herring. Australian herring are so named because the fish look similar to herring found in the Northern Hemisphere but they are perch and are native to Australian waters. Tommy ruff are great pan fried, grilled or simply marinated; they have a rustic white flesh that is perfect served with lemon juice and salt. If marinated fish is not your cup of tea, simply follow the recipe then briefly fry the fillets skin side down until crisp and golden and serve, cooking the fish on one side only.

8 x 60 g (2 oz) tommy ruff fillets
Salt and pepper
2 tablespoons yuzu juice (or juice of ½ orange or 1 lemon)
1 tablespoon olive oil
2 tablespoons Curry Oil (see page 25) (optional)

BROCCOLI COUSCOUS
2 medium broccoli heads
2 tablespoons extra-virgin olive oil
1 shallot, finely chopped
1 garlic clove, finely crushed
80 g (3 oz) pine nuts, roasted
80 g (3 oz) baby sultanas

CARROT DRESSING
100 ml (3½ fl oz) fresh carrot juice
25 ml (1 fl oz) Champagne vinegar
100 ml (3½ fl oz) extra-virgin olive oil

Remove bones or scales from the fish and put fillets into a medium-sized bowl. Add salt, pepper, yuzu juice and 1 tablespoon olive oil. Leave to marinate for 30 minutes.

BROCCOLI COUSCOUS

1   With a sharp knife, shave the flowers off the top of the broccoli to obtain the texture and appearance of couscous.

2   Shave the stem very thinly into ribbons using a mandolin. Slice and blanch the ribbons in boiling water until they are just tender.

3   Toss the ribbons with a little olive oil in a bowl. Add the shallot, shaved broccoli, garlic, pine nuts and sultanas. Taste and adjust seasoning if necessary. Spoon the salad evenly onto 4 plates.

CARROT DRESSING

1 Put the carrot juice into a heavy-based saucepan over medium heat and reduce by half. Add the vinegar a little at a time and taste: it should be sweet and acidic, reminiscent of sweet and sour.

2 Chill in a stainless steel bowl over ice, or in the refrigerator, then whisk in the 100 ml (3½ fl oz) extra-virgin olive oil.

TO SERVE

Place the fish fillets on the top of the broccoli and drizzle the carrot dressing around and over the fish. Dot the plate with curry oil if desired.

* NOTE *
Curry oil is used in the recipe: you can follow the instructions on page 25, or to make a quick version, toast some curry powder in a heavy-based pan over medium heat, add some olive oil and stir to combine. Strain to remove the powder and use as required.

CONFIT OF OCEAN TROUT WITH GINGER JUS

SERVES 6

Ocean trout is very easy to overcook, but I have found a way – after many years of trial and error – to teach young chefs how to cook this very popular, farmed fish properly. Confiting the fish, submerging it in a bath of oil at a low temperature, gives ample time for the cook to observe the chemical changes of the proteins as they develop from raw, to translucent, to cooked. In layman's terms, this technique demonstrates well how the fish is just cooked in the centre but also has a pleasing and appetising overall look. The ginger sauce can accompany any seafood with great results. Salmon can be used in this recipe instead of ocean trout.

1 litre (2 pints) extra-virgin olive oil
6 x 250 g (9 oz) ocean trout or salmon fillets

GINGER SAUCE
4 tablespoons finely sliced ginger
1 tablespoon thinly sliced garlic
3 tablespoons thinly sliced spring onions, white
    part only
250 ml (8½ fl oz) Chinese cooking wine
600 ml (20 fl oz) Chicken Stock (see page 17),
    reduced to 300 ml (10 fl oz)
2 tablespoons oyster sauce
2 tablespoons light mushroom soy sauce
1 small fennel bulb, thinly sliced
3 tablespoons julienned spring onions,
    green part only

1 Fill a heatproof dish about 20 x 20 cm (8 x 8 in) and at least 10 cm (3 in) deep with the olive oil and heat to a temperature of 60°C (140°F) over low heat.

2 Add the trout and leave for 10 minutes, or until fish is almost transparent.

3 Remove the trout with a fish slice and place each fillet in the centre of a warm plate.

4 Take 3 tablespoons of the olive oil used to cook the trout and put in a saucepan over a medium heat. Add the ginger and fry (you need to hear the ginger sizzling) for 1 minute – the ginger should not become coloured at all. Add sliced garlic and fry for 30 seconds. Add the white spring onions and fry for 30 seconds.

5 Add Chinese wine and reduce its volume over heat by two-thirds. Add the chicken stock, bring to the boil and whisk in the oyster and soy sauces. Add fennel and julienned green spring onion to the sauce and serve immediately, pouring over the trout.

SARDINES ON TOAST

SERVES 4

I have dedicated this recipe to my wife and child as it is our family favourite on a Sunday night. Simple to prepare, it also makes great finger food when friends are around for drinks.

Juice of ½ lemon
1 garlic clove, crushed
50 ml (2 fl oz) olive oil
Sea salt and pepper
16 butterflied sardines
1 teaspoon finely chopped flat-leaf parsley
8 slices white sourdough bread
8 tablespoons extra-virgin olive oil
16 slices buffalo mozzarella or 16 bocconcini, halved
8 tablespoons Tomato Fondue (see page 18)
Additional extra-virgin olive oil
Handful of rocket leaves

1 Preheat the oven to 180°C (350°F), and also preheat the grill.

2 Combine the lemon juice, garlic, olive oil and salt and pepper in a bowl. Add the sardines, and leave to marinate in the liquid for 15 minutes.

3 Add the chopped parsley and gently mix it with the sardines, using your fingertips.

4 Brush the sourdough bread with olive oil on both sides and grill, then season with salt and pepper.

5 Put the toasted sourdough in an oven tray. Place 2 slices of the mozzarella on each piece of sourdough. Spoon over tomato fondue, then place 2 butterflied sardines on top.

6 Put into the oven for 4 minutes or until warm.

7 Before serving, drizzle with extra-virgin olive oil and season with sea salt and ground pepper. Serve with fresh rocket leaves around and on top of the sardines.

Sardines on toast makes
great finger food when friends
are around for drinks.

SQUID PROVENCALE

SERVES 4

Squid is often overlooked by most people when buying in a fish shop but I hope this recipe will encourage you to try it, so you realise how simple, tasty and delicate this wonderful cephalopod really is. The recipe can be interpreted with any sort of seafood, even with meat or vegetables. I like to use these ingredients and method with lamb fillets, but add crushed anchovies when sautéing the vegetables.

1 eggplant
2 red capsicums (bell peppers)
1 zucchini
1 red onion
Olive oil
250 ml (8½ fl oz) Tomato Fondue (see page 18)
250 ml (8½ fl oz) white wine
50 g (2 oz) black olives, pitted and halved
Salt and pepper
4 x 250 g (9 oz) calamari tubes with tentacles,
    cleaned
Juice of ½ lemon
4 tablespoons Persillage (see page 142) (optional)
Handful of basil leaves

l   Remove the black skin from the eggplant with a peeler, leaving about 5 mm (¼ in) of flesh on the skin. Cut the skin into 2 cm (¾ in) dice. Reserve the inner flesh for Baba Ghanoush (see page 40).

2   Dice the zucchini, capsicum and red onion into 2 cm (¾ in) dice.

3   In a hot frying pan, sauté the vegetables, including eggplant skin, in olive oil until tender. Add the tomato fondue and the white wine, simmer for 2–3 minutes. Add the olives to the vegetables. Season to taste.

4   Heat a chargrill or griddle pan until smoking. Toss the calamari in olive oil and salt. Place on the hot grill until charred on one side, turn over to char the other side (this should only take a minute). Squeeze over the lemon juice and remove from the heat, place in a bowl and season.

5   To serve, place the cooked vegetables with their sauce in shallow serving bowls. Place the calamari on top and sprinkle liberally with the persillage. Scatter the basil leaves on top and serve immediately.

MARINATED PRAWNS WITH CAULIFLOWER COUSCOUS   SERVES 4

I do not use farmed products much but I have fallen for a product that has benefited from farming – Crystal Bay prawns. They seem to be the only fresh prawn sold in the Melbourne market and their flavour is amazing. They are small but very easy to peel and the shells make the best shellfish stock known to man. Cauliflower couscous is obviously not couscous as such but has the same texture as cracked wheat. I have taken the idea from Ferran Adrià, who would have to be one of the most humble and nicest chefs I have ever met. The dish does involve a little patience and preparation before cooking but the work is essential; the oils can be made well in advance.

32 small green prawns (shrimp), peeled
200 ml (7 fl oz) Curry Oil (see page 25)
200 ml (7 fl oz) Crayfish Oil (see page 25)
2 garlic cloves, crushed
Salt and pepper
200 ml (7 fl oz) rice wine
300 ml (10 fl oz) fish stock
¼ cauliflower
1 tablespoon olive oil
30 g (1 oz) pine nuts, toasted
30 g (1 oz) sultanas
2 chives, chopped
Juice of ½ lemon
100 g (3½ oz) cultured butter, diced

1 Marinate the prawns in the oils, garlic, salt and pepper for 30 minutes.

2 Put the rice wine and fish stock into a saucepan and bring to the boil over a medium heat. Place a steaming basket over the boiling stock.

3 Put the prawns into the basket and cover with a lid, steam for about 3–4 minutes, then remove the basket from the heat.

4 Add any remaining marinating liquid to the stock and reduce it by two-thirds.

5 Trim the cauliflower into tiny florets. A quick way is to use a coarse grater.

6 Put florets into a food processor and pulse until cauliflower looks like couscous.

7 In a frying pan, on a medium heat, sauté the cauliflower in the olive oil. Add pine nuts, sultanas and chives and continue to sauté for another 2 minutes but don't completely cook the cauliflower. Take off the heat and season to taste, set aside until ready to serve.

8 Whisk the butter into the reduced fish sauce until thoroughly incorporated, remove from the heat.

9 On individual plates, first place a pile of couscous. Arrange the prawns on and around the couscous, spoon the sauce over them and serve.

BOUILLABAISSE RISOTTO

Bouillabaisse has to be included in a cookery book based on traditional French cuisine. The stock can become a soup with the addition of fish or shellfish and diced root vegetables added moments before serving. Carnaroli rice comes from Novara and Vercelli in the Piedmonte Valley, Europe's largest rice-growing area. Carnaroli, arborio and vialone nano – fashionable with many chefs at the moment – are similar varieties with short, plump grains and the high starch content that gives risotto its characteristic creaminess. I feel I make the best risotto with carnaroli because it is slightly drier than one made with the smaller-grained vialone nano. I prefer the Ferron brand, available from good providores.

SEAFOOD STOCK

10 x 80 g (3 oz) red mullet carcasses (eyes removed)

500 g (1 lb 2 oz) crab, lobster or crustacean shells

5 over-ripe roma (plum) tomatoes

1 carrot, 1 celery stalk and 1 onion, all diced

1 head of garlic, chopped in half

2 bay leaves

2 pinches of saffron

4 star anise

500 ml (1 pint) dry white wine

150 ml (5 fl oz) pastis (Pernod)

150 g (5 oz) tomato paste

250 ml (8½ fl oz) extra-virgin olive oil

Salt and pepper

2 litres (4 pints) fish stock plus 500 ml (1 pint) mussel stock or 2.5 litres (5 pints) water

RISOTTO

2 tablespoons olive oil

1 onion, finely diced

250 g (9 oz) Ferron carnaroli rice

250 ml (8½ fl oz) white wine

4 tablespoons grated Grana Padano cheese

4 tablespoons cultured butter

Juice of ½ lemon

Salt and freshly ground black pepper

SQUID GARNISH

4 baby squid with tentacles, cleaned

Plain (all purpose) flour, seasoned with salt and pepper

Juice of 1 lemon

SEAFOOD STOCK

1 Combine the bones and shells with vegetables, herbs, spices, wine, pastis, tomato paste and half the olive oil in a large container. Cover and marinate in the refrigerator for 12–24 hours.

2 Strain contents and set both solids and marinade aside. Heat remaining olive oil in a heavy-based saucepan, add bones, shells and vegetables. Cook for 4–5 minutes, until bones are golden. Season. Add reserved marinade and reduce over low heat until evaporated. Add the 2.5 litres (5 pints) liquid and simmer for 2 hours.

3 Using a hand blender, roughly purée the stock – don't worry about the bones and shells. Pass it through a coarse sieve, then a fine sieve. Discard solids. Reserve stock in an airtight container in the refrigerator; it can also be frozen for 3 months. You may find an orange oil separates from it; whisk this back into the stock before using as its flavour is essential.

RISOTTO

1   Just cover the bottom of a medium-sized heavy-based pot with olive oil and heat. Once oil is hot, add onion and cook until translucent. Add rice and stir to coat in oil; cook for a further 2 minutes. Add wine and cook until it has been absorbed (about 5 minutes). Then add hot seafood stock 1 cup at a time, occasionally stirring gently, allowing liquid to be absorbed before adding more. Continue until rice is tender. While rice is cooking, prepare squid (see below).

2   Remove rice from heat; add cheese, butter, a squeeze of lemon, to taste, and season. Stir slowly to emulsify the cheese and butter evenly through the rice, being careful not to crush the grains. Adjust the texture of the rice, particularly if it has become gluggy, with a little more hot stock.

SQUID

1   Preheat vegetable oil in a deep fryer or large heavy-based saucepan to 180°C (350°F).

2   Cut the squid tubes into strips. Lightly flour tubes and tentacles, shaking off excess. Deep-fry squid until golden brown. Drain on absorbent paper and season with salt, pepper and lemon juice. Keep warm.

TO SERVE

Divide risotto between warm flat bowls or plates. Arrange fried squid on top of the risotto and serve immediately.

Meat

THE PERFECT STEAK
SERVES 4

My preference is to cook steak on a barbecue or grill with heat beads as I find this creates a lovely smokiness and associated characteristics of a great steak – juicy and packed full of texture. The three cuts that respond best to this type of rustic cooking are porterhouse, scotch fillet and rump. Always choose meat that is full of fatty marbling and dark in colour. The colour is a particularly good indicator of whether the joint has been aged correctly.

4 x 250 g (9 oz) rump steaks
Sea salt and cracked black pepper
4 tablespoons extra-virgin olive oil or goose fat
   or beef fat
1 teaspoon sherry vinegar

1 Preheat a barbecue or grill with heat beads, to a medium heat. Season the steaks well with cracked pepper and sea salt. Drizzle plenty of olive oil or fat onto the steaks.

2 Place on the grill and leave for 3 minutes, turn over and cook for a further 3 minutes.

3 For rare steak remove from the grill now and rest on a warm plate or tray for 6 minutes before serving. For medium steak, cook on each side for a further minute; for well-done steak, cook on each side for a further 3 minutes. In each case, rest off the heat for 8–10 minutes before serving.

4 Before serving, make a simple sauce from the resting juices by pouring the juices into a bowl, add the sherry vinegar and 2 tablespoons of olive oil or melted beef fat. Spoon this over the steak before serving. Alternatively, serve with Green Peppercorn Sauce.

GREEN PEPPERCORN SAUCE
SERVES 4

Every pub in Australia has something in common with every bistro in France: peppercorn sauce. The only difference is the French are much more resourceful with this simple and wonderful sauce by serving it with a wider range of meats, not just steak. My favourite is either with confit duck leg or roast venison. I also much prefer to use brown chicken stock rather than normal stock, as it has a greater depth of flavour.

500 ml (1 pint) Brown Chicken Stock (page 17) or
   Veal Stock (page 16)
200 g (7 oz) green peppercorns in brine
1 tablespoon finely chopped parsley
30 g (1 oz) cultured butter
Salt and pepper

1 Bring the stock to the boil. Add the drained peppercorns, infuse for 5 minutes by gently simmering in the stock. Add the parsley and butter, whisk for 30 seconds or until the butter has melted into the sauce.

2 Taste and season accordingly. Serve immediately with your perfectly cooked steak.

ROAST BEEF WITH YORKSHIRE PUDDINGS

Yorkshire pudding is one of the toughest recipes in the business. Thankfully my time in England served me well, as I was fortunate enough to learn from John Burton Race what a good 'Yorky' was. The recipe below will make 4–6, depending on the size of the moulds. Any fat or oil can be substituted for the goose fat, as long as it is smoking before you drop the batter in. Wagyu beef with a marble score of 3–5 is now available from specialist butchers.

1 kg (2 lb 3 oz) piece wagyu sirloin, marble score
  3–5, rolled and tied
Salt and freshly ground black pepper
150 ml (5 fl oz) olive oil
1 head of garlic, halved across
1 small carrot, roughly chopped
1 celery stalk, roughly chopped
1 leek, white part only, roughly chopped
8 sprigs of thyme
2 bay leaves
100 g (3½ oz) cultured butter
200 ml (7 fl oz) red wine
500 ml (1 pint) Veal Stock (see page 16)
1 quantity Béarnaise Sauce (see page 14)

YORKSHIRE PUDDINGS
200 g (7 oz) plain (all-purpose) flour
200 ml (7 fl oz) milk
100 ml (3½ fl oz) water
5 eggs
½ teaspoon baking powder
Salt to taste
10 tablespoons goose fat

PUDDING BATTER

Put the flour, milk, water, eggs and baking powder in a large bowl and mix with a hand-held blender for 3–4 minutes, until a smooth, aerated batter forms. Add salt and mix. Rest batter, preferably overnight but for at least 1 hour.

ROAST BEEF

1 Preheat the oven to 180°C (350°F). Put a large roasting tray over medium–high heat on top of the stove.

2 Generously season the beef all over. When the tray is hot, add the oil and then the beef. Pan-roast beef for 2–3 minutes until dark and caramelised on one side, then turn it to colour on all sides. Add the vegetables to the tray, cook until they have a little colour, then add herbs. Spoon tray juices over the meat.

3 Roast in oven for around 45 minutes for medium-rare to medium (the temperature of domestic ovens is often inaccurate, so adjust cooking time to taste).

4 Remove the tray from the oven, cover beef with foil and rest the meat for about 20 minutes in a warm place.

YORKSHIRE PUDDINGS

1 As soon as you remove the beef, increase the oven temperature to 200°C (400°F). Use a non-stick muffin tin and put a tablespoon of fat in each mould. Heat in oven for 20 minutes or until the oil is smoking.

2 Pour batter into the centre of each mould until half full. Repeat quickly (to retain heat in the tray) until tray is full and bake in oven for about 20 minutes. Remove from oven when the puddings are crisp, golden and doubled in size.

TO SERVE

1 Once beef has rested, remove it from the tray, keeping it warm. Strain the meat juices and reserve. Put pan with vegetables over medium heat on the stove, add the butter, briefly sauté vegetables. Deglaze the pan with the wine, scraping the caramelised pieces off the base; reduce the liquid by two-thirds, then add stock and reduce by half.

2 Return the reserved meat juices to the tray and simmer to a consistency similar to a light gravy. Strain it through a fine sieve, discard solids, and keep warm until required.

3 Slice the beef and arrange on warmed plates, with two or three Yorkshire puddings per plate, a generous spoon of Pea Purée (see page 162) and a dollop of Béarnaise Sauce. Finish by drizzling the gravy into the Yorkshire puddings.

Oxtail takes a long time to cook so if you use another cut, scale back the timing, depending on the amount of sinew the meat you choose contains.

POT AU FEU

The phrase 'pot au feu' is derived from the older French *pot pourri*, a dish of ox meat, asparagus, artichokes and mushrooms which were boiled together with aromatic herbs in a basic stock and served to notables at the royal court. From this beginning, a very traditional, bourgeois recipe has been recorded by chefs and writers over the past three centuries in many forms. Oxtail is my preferred meat for this dish because of its generous flavour and gelatine but feel free to experiment with any cut you wish.

4 oxtails, cut into 4 pieces
2 turnips, quartered
2 large carrots, cut into large pieces
1 onion, diced
8 garlic cloves, bruised
8 Jerusalem artichokes (around golfball size),
   unpeeled
2 celery stalks, cut into 3 pieces
4 bay leaves
6 sprigs of thyme
2 litres (5 pints) Chicken Stock (see page 17)
Salt and pepper
1 quantity Pizza Dough (see page 22)

1 Preheat the oven to 160°C (320°F).

2 Place all the ingredients in the order listed except the dough into a large casserole dish, minimum size about 6 litres (12 pints). Season well.

3 Put the lid on the pot and cook in the oven for 6 hours.

4 Remove the pot from the oven and taste, adjust seasoning accordingly. Rest the meat until cool enough to handle the oxtail. Remove all the oxtail and pick the meat away from the bones. Return the meat to the pot, discarding the bones.

5 Seal the lid with pizza dough by rolling the dough into a large sausage and wrapping around the pot over the seal between the pot and lid. Place back in the oven for 30 minutes.

6 Serve with Parsley Pommes Mousseline (see page 159).

WAGYU BEEF WITH MUSHROOM FONDUE

Fondues are very popular in China. I first came across this really social, family way of eating at a Hong Kong restaurant where stoves were built into each table and you chose your combination of ingredients from a large menu. The extensive marbling in wagyu beef is very well suited to this style of cooking. This recipe is good with Braised Lentils (see page 160).

400 g (14 oz) grade 6–12 wagyu beef sirloin,
   fat removed
800 ml (28 fl oz) Mushroom Stock (see page 24)
50 g (2 oz) dried trumpet mushrooms
2 tablespoons finely diced shallots
1 tablespoon finely chopped parsley
4 handfuls baby spinach, washed
Salt and freshly ground black pepper

1 Slice the beef as thinly as possible and lay neatly on a plate, slightly overlapping each piece.

2 Bring the mushroom stock to the boil, add the other ingredients except seasoning and boil over a high heat for 2 minutes, then season to taste. Ladle the stock and its contents evenly into 4 very hot deep serving bowls.

3 Serve the beef in the middle of the table and accompany each bowl of stock with a pair of chopsticks. Dip slices of beef into the hot stock and eat quickly.

NOTES ON WAGYU

Grade 12 marbling, the best grade of wagyu, has become more readily available. The reason is that, until recently, the wagyu cattle industry in Australia consisted of production of F1 and F2 hybrid crosses for the Japanese and South-East Asian markets. An F1 is a cross between a wagyu sire and another breed of cattle, often Angus, though Holstein and Murray Grey are proving popular. An F2 animal is the result of the cross of a wagyu sire with an F1 female. Now the domestic wagyu industry has begun to release highly sought-after full-blood wagyu, which has exceptional marbling and flavour that rivals the finest wagyu available in Japan.

VEAL HOLSTEIN

Veal is a touchy subject amongst chefs, who disagree about which qualities give the best result. I prefer a darker meat when choosing veal at the butcher as I think it has a richer, sweeter taste. Most classically trained chefs prefer a lighter, paler flesh that sacrifices flavour for delicate texture. Friedrich von Holstein, by the way, was a German diplomat under Bismarck who requested a new way of eating veal whilst dining at Café Anglaise in Paris.

4 x 150 g (5 oz) veal loin steaks
Salt and freshly ground black pepper
100 g (3½ oz) plain (all purpose) flour
2 eggs, lightly beaten
100 g (3½ oz) panko breadcrumbs
50 ml (12 fl oz) olive oil, plus extra for cooking
8 small eggs (either small hen's eggs or pigeon's)
8 anchovy fillets
200 g (7 oz) spinach, washed
2 tablespoons chopped parsley
Juice of ½ lemon
4–6 tablespoons Béarnaise Sauce (see page 14)

1 Place veal steaks on a chopping board and cover with heavy plastic. Tenderise veal using a mallet, remove plastic and season meat.

2 Put flour, eggs and breadcrumbs in separate bowls. Dip each veal fillet first in the flour – ensuring that it is lightly covered and shaking off excess – then in beaten egg, again shaking off excess, and finally in breadcrumbs. Put the crumbed fillets on a tray and refrigerate until required.

3 Gently heat some olive oil in a non-stick frying pan. Add the eggs, cooking gently so they do not fry but instead are warmed through and are 'confited' in the oil, until the whites are set. Carefully remove from the pan with a fish slice and place on a plate lined with absorbent paper to drain excess oil. Trim whites neatly with a circular cutter, then cross 2 anchovies on top of each egg.

4 Heat a heavy-based frying pan over medium heat. Fry the spinach in a hot pan with a little more olive oil. When wilted drain on absorbent paper or a tea towel.

5 Warm the plates for serving.

6 Heat a large non-stick frying pan over medium heat, add the olive oil and gently place the veal in the pan one at a time. Fry until golden (approximately 1 minute), then flip over to fry the other side for a further minute. Pour the lemon juice over the veal and scatter parsley on top.

7 Dollop some béarnaise sauce on each plate. Divide the spinach, place a veal fillet on top of the spinach and 2 eggs on top of each fillet.

HAY-SMOKED LAMB GALETTE

The hay adds a unique smoked flavour to the lamb, whilst the galette keeps the shoulder meat moist. This recipe cannot be described as 'simple', but the result is well worth the effort. The galette method can be adapted to any type of braised meat. A good deal of preparation can be done the day before you intend to serve.

GALETTE
2 sheets puff pastry, 15 x 15 cm and 2.5 cm thick
  (6 x 6 in, ½ in thick)
2 tablespoons stock from Braised Lamb
1 tablespoon chopped shallots
1 tablespoon sherry vinegar
1 tablespoon chopped parsley
1 teaspoon garlic purée
Salt and pepper

BRAISED LAMB
600 ml (20 fl oz) Veal Stock (see page 16)
125 ml (4 fl oz) white wine
500 g (1 lb 2 oz) diced lamb shoulder

LAMB RACK
1 x 4 point lamb rack (weighing about 300 g/10 oz)
Salt and pepper

CRUSHED PEAS
500 g (1 lb 2 oz) peas
Salt and pepper
2 tablespoons chopped shallots
1 tablespoon cultured butter

TO SERVE
1 handful of hay/straw (optional)
150 g (5 oz) plain (all purpose) flour
2 eggs, lightly beaten
150 g (5 oz) panko breadcrumbs
2 tablespoons olive oil
1 bunch of English watercress (optional)

1 Preheat the oven to 180°C (350°F).

2 Put the pastry on a tray lined with baking paper; put another sheet of paper over then another tray on top. Bake for 25 minutes or until golden and crisp. Carefully place the pastry on a wire rack to cool.

BRAISED LAMB

1 Turn the oven down to 140°C (275°F).

2 Put the stock and wine in a medium, heavy-based pot, bring to the boil and add lamb. Cover pot tightly with foil and a lid. Bake 3–4 hours, until meat is tender.

3 Rest for 30 minutes to cool. Remove lamb from the braise with a slotted spoon, pick through it and discard fat or bones. Strain braising stock through a fine strainer into a saucepan, set aside.

GALETTE

1 Put lamb in a large bowl with 2 tablespoons stock and all galette seasonings. Mix well but do not break the meat up too much.

2 Take a dish about 15 x 15 cm and 5–6 cm deep (6 x 6 in, 2 in deep); cut baking paper to fit the bottom. Place a sheet of cooked pastry on the paper; top with lamb mixture, about 2.5 cm (1 in) thick. Top with another sheet of pastry, cover with baking paper and press down using a heavy weight. Refrigerate for 1–2 hours, until firm. Then neatly cut galette into quarters.

CRUSHED PEAS

Bring a pan of water to a rapid boil and add peas: if frozen cook for 2 minutes, if fresh for 6 minutes. Strain peas, put into a bowl, crush with a fork, add salt, pepper, shallot and butter.

The recipe can be prepared to this point the day before.

TO SERVE

1 Heat the oven to 180°C (350°F).

2 Heat a heavy-based skillet or ovenproof frying pan over medium heat. Season the rack well and cook until caramelised on all sides. When golden, remove meat and add a handful of fresh hay to pan. After 4–5 minutes the hay will start to smoke, then place the rack resting on the bone back in the pan, move to oven and roast for 8–10 minutes.

3 Remove from oven. Rest the meat for 5–6 minutes in a warm place. Discard hay.

4 Crumb galettes: coat them in flour, dip in beaten egg then into breadcrumbs. Repeat for all galettes twice.

5 Add a tablespoon of oil to the pan over medium heat, and cook galettes all over until golden, then bake in oven for 5 minutes at 180°C (350°F).

6 While the galettes cook, simmer braising stock over low heat for 2–3 minutes (if you feel it is too thin, reduce it further to a sauce consistency). Season. Heat the crushed peas.

7 Dollop crushed peas in the centre of each plate, sit a lamb galette on the top. Carve rack into cutlets and rest one on each galette. Pour sauce over the top and finish with a sprinkle of watercress.

LAMB CHOPS WITH APPLE CIDER

SERVES 4

Households of Australia and, in fact, the world, listen! Using flavourful wine and brandy in cooking is good, it makes food come alive, even simple old lamb chops – and the way things are going there will be no such thing as 'simple old' anything when it comes to meat, as prices will soar as people become more conscious of how they would like their produce to be treated and the effects of global warming make farming more expensive. I can cook this dish at home within two glasses of wine being consumed so don't feel daunted as this is one of the easiest recipes to produce from the cupboard to the plate.

12 lamb cutlets

Salt and pepper

2 tablespoons finely chopped sage leaves

50 g (2 oz) plain (all purpose) flour

4 eggs, beaten

200 g (7 oz) stale sourdough bread, broken into
    small pieces and left to dry out overnight

12 kipfler potatoes

8 baby fennel

200 ml (7 fl oz) olive oil, for frying

50 g (2 oz) shallots, chopped

2 tablespoons finely chopped parsley

180 ml (6 fl oz) flat apple cider

60 ml (2½ fl oz) Calvados (optional)

100 g (3½ oz) cultured butter

1 Crumb the lamb chops: first season them well with salt and pepper and a sprinkle of sage, then dip the chops into the flour, followed by the beaten egg and then into the dried sourdough crumbs. Set chops aside.

2 Top and tail the kipfler potatoes, then with a small turning knife use a peeling action to shape the potato into a 7-sided barrel: this is called a 'château' potato.

3 Cook the potatoes in salted boiling water for approximately 6 minutes, until tender, but be careful not to let them break up. Drain potatoes and set aside.

4 Bring another saucepan of salted water to the boil. Top and tail the baby fennel, add to the water and cook for 2 minutes, drain and set aside.

5 Put a heavy-based skillet over a high heat, add some olive oil to the pan and shallow-fry the chops, 4 at a time. Cook for 2 minutes on each side or until golden then remove from the pan and place on a tray lined with absorbent paper. Repeat until all the chops are cooked.

6 Once completed, remove the oil from the pan, wipe it clean and put it back on the heat. Add 1 tablespoon of olive oil and sauté the shallots for 30 seconds, then add the chops, potatoes, fennel and parsley and sauté for a further minute.

7 Add the cider and deglaze, and then add the Calvados (if using) and flambé, heating to reduce the liquor rapidly, then add the butter, and season well.

Each person will have 3 chops, 3 potatoes and 2 baby fennel, on their plate; spoon over the pan juices and serve.

POT-ROAST PORK BELLY WITH CALVADOS, BLACK PUDDING AND APPLE

SERVES 4

The origins of this recipe remind me of the dishes that one would find in Southern Ireland or Normandy, but to my surprise I had not come across a combination of these flavours until I discovered them whilst working for John Burton Race's L'Ortolan in the mid-1990s; I still draw inspiration today in my own menus from his mastery of apples, Calvados and pork. The pork belly is best braised in chicken stock with vegetables for three hours the day before serving, for the ultimate result, but leftover roast pork is suitable for this recipe also.

12 pieces cooked pork belly (about 50 g/2 oz each)

12 slices black pudding (about 20 g/¾ oz each), dusted in flour

50 g (2 oz) duck or chicken fat

3 Granny Smith apples, peeled, cored and cut into 12 wedges

1 onion, finely diced

2 garlic cloves, crushed

100 ml (3½ fl oz) Calvados

50 g (2 oz) cultured butter

1 tablespoon finely chopped flat-leaf parsley

Salt and pepper

1 Place the pork in a hot skillet or heavy-based pan at least 30 cm (12 in) in diameter over a medium heat. Cook the pork briefly on all sides until golden. Caution should be taken to avoid being burnt from the pork fat spitting whilst in the pan – put a piece of foil loosely over the top of the pan.

2 Remove the pork and drain well on absorbent paper. Keep the pan hot and return the drained pork to the pan. Add the well-dusted black pudding, cook for 1–2 minutes over high heat, turning the black pudding halfway through; add the duck or chicken fat as needed.

3 Add the apple to the black pudding and continue to pan roast over a high heat. Add the onion and garlic and carefully stir, being careful not to break up the black pudding.

4 Add the Calvados, tilt the pan towards the flame to ignite the Calvados and burn off the alcohol. Turn the heat down to medium and simmer for 2 minutes, add the butter and parsley, toss and season well with salt and pepper.

5 Serve with Parsley Pommes Mousseline (page 159) and Watercress and Hazelnut Salad (page 99) or a garden salad. Braised cabbage is another great accompaniment.

Apples, Calvados and pork are a great combination of flavours.

The true definition of a cassoulet is a stew that contains haricot blanc beans and some form of meat.

PORK, FENNEL, POTATO AND SAFFRON CASSOULET   SERVES 4

Classical cassoulet is interpreted in many ways and this recipe is my version. The true definition of a cassoulet is a stew that contains haricot blanc beans and some form of meat, and is braised traditionally in a sealed earthenware pot for many hours. This recipe can be easily adapted to a vegetarian version by replacing the meat with your favourite root vegetables and the chicken stock with vegetable stock. Merguez sausages are mildly spicy sausages made with lamb.

200 g (7 oz) haricot beans
1 tablespoon goose fat
1 Bouquet Garni (see page 21)
250 g (9 oz) diced pork belly or smoked bacon
2 shallots, peeled and finely sliced
3 garlic cloves, thinly sliced
Pinch of saffron
200 ml (7 fl oz) white wine
500 ml (1 pint) Chicken Stock (see page 17),
    heated until boiling
12 golfball-sized baby carrots
500 g (1 lb 2 oz) fennel, cubed
4 merguez lamb sausages
20 small kipfler or ratte potatoes, peeled
2 teaspoons salt and pepper

1 Soak the haricot beans in cold water for 12 hours in the refrigerator.

2 Put the beans in a heavy-based pot over a medium heat and simmer in water for 1 hour or until the beans have absorbed most of the water. Set aside.

3 In a large heavy-based pot (large enough to hold all the ingredients) put the goose fat, bouquet garni, diced pork belly, shallots, garlic and saffron. Cook slowly, stirring consistently, until the shallots are tender.

4 Add the white wine and reduce the wine until all the liquid has evaporated. Add boiling chicken stock to the pot. Add the haricot beans, cover with a lid and simmer until the pork is tender (about 2 hours).

5 Add carrots, diced fennel, sausages and potatoes. Season with salt and pepper.

6 Preheat the oven to 140°C (275°F). Put the casserole into the oven.

7 Allow crust to form and break the crust eight times during cooking – which will take about 3 hours.

8 Serve at your leisure with crusty bread.

ROAST CHICKEN

The herbed breadcrumbs combined with the simple sauce take this dish into the realms of restaurant quality. I make no apology for serving my meat warm, not piping hot like my grandmother used to. No offence to my Nan, but meat that is piping hot has lost a lot of moisture and with it a lot of flavour; don't reheat this chicken once you have taken it off the bone. Note that some preparation is needed the day before you intend to serve the dish.

1 free-range chicken, about 1.5–2 kg (3–4½ lb)
500 g (1 lb 2 oz) goose fat
Salt and pepper
12 kipfler potatoes
2 tablespoons cultured butter
8 shallots
1 head of garlic, broken into cloves
8 baby turnips
8 Dutch carrots
8 sprigs of thyme
100 ml (3½ fl oz) Madeira
100 ml (3½ fl oz) water

PERSILLAGE (HERBED BREADCRUMBS)

2 tablespoons finely chopped curly-leaf parsley
1 teaspoon fresh thyme leaves
2 garlic cloves
4 tablespoons olive oil
50 g (2 oz) panko breadcrumbs

THE DAY BEFORE

Preheat oven to 140°C (275°F). Remove the chicken neck, wishbone, wing tips and legs. Put all chicken except the legs back into the refrigerator. Preheat goose fat to 120°C (250°F) in an ovenproof pot with a lid. Season legs, then add to the fat, cover lightly with foil, put lid on and bake for 1–1½ hours or until the meat starts to fall off the bone. Remove from oven, allow to cool in the fat, then refrigerate.

TO COMPLETE COOKING

1 Preheat oven to 180°C (350°F).

2 Make the persillage: put parsley, thyme, garlic, olive oil and crumbs in a processor and pulse until mix is fine. Set aside.

3 Put potatoes into a pan of cold water, salt well and boil until soft, about 15 minutes. To check if they are ready push a small knife into the flesh of one: it should enter without resistance. Drain potatoes, cool for 5–10 minutes, then peel off skins.

4 While the potatoes are cooking, put chicken on a board with the neck towards you. With poultry scissors or a sharp knife, remove the underside of the bird, leaving the breasts (crown). Chop backbone, neck and wing tips into 5 cm (2 in) pieces; put in a baking tray and set aside.

5 Run fingertips carefully under the skin of the breast, starting at the neck, separating skin from meat. Take a large handful of persillage and fill the cavity between meat and skin completely. Rub butter over the skin. Place chicken on the bones in the tray, season well. Toss potatoes, shallots and garlic generously in goose fat, season well and add to tray. Cover it tightly with foil, roast for 1 hour.

6 Wash turnips and carrots well. Toss with thyme and a generous amount of goose fat, season. Add these to the roasting tray 15 minutes before crown is ready. At intervals during roasting, remove foil and ladle fat from the confit pot containing legs over the bird.

7 After 1 hour, remove tray from oven, put crown on a plate, cover with foil and rest in a warm place.

8 Put a heavy-based frying pan over medium heat. Add chicken legs, season well and cook for 2–3 minutes until crisp on the skin side. Drain well on absorbent paper and rest under foil with the crown.

9 Put all vegetables on a warm serving plate, leaving bones in tray. Drain any fat from tray and reserve. Place it over medium heat; once the sediment on the bottom starts to colour, deglaze with Madeira and reduce, stirring and scraping to impart all the flavour into the Madeira. Reduce volume by two-thirds, add water, return to the boil and reduce for a further 2 minutes. Strain into a saucepan, season to taste: the sauce should resemble thin gravy. Add 2–3 tablespoons of the chicken fat to it. Do not stir.

10 Remove warm breasts from the bone and cut into 4 equal pieces. Halve the legs. Arrange chicken in the centre of each dinner plate, with garlic, shallots, turnips and carrots around the meat, then spoon sauce over and around the chicken.

Quails make a suitable alternative if baby chickens are not available.

COQ AU VIN: BABY CHICKEN BRAISED IN SWEET WINE WITH BABY VEGETABLES

SERVES 2

Baby chickens, or poussin, are a little out of vogue at the moment but I love their delicate flavour and convenience when cooking for two. As you can tell from many of my recipes, I am a one-pot man in my kitchen as I hate cleaning up and I hate to leave the mess for my wife! This dish goes well with a good crisp Gewürztraminer.

1 x 600 g (1 lb 5 oz) free-range chicken
4 baby carrots, peeled
8 baby onions, peeled
8 garlic cloves
8 baby beetroots
6 sprigs of tarragon
375 ml (13 fl oz) sweet white wine
2 tablespoons cultured butter
500 ml (1 pint) sparkling mineral water
Salt and pepper

1 Preheat the oven to 180°C (350°F).

2 Put all the ingredients into a copper or ceramic pot with a suitable lid and bring to the boil on the stove over a high heat. Remove from the heat and cover the pot tightly with aluminium foil before placing the lid on. Cook in the oven for 2½ hours.

3 Remove from the oven and rest for 10 minutes. Taste and adjust the seasoning as necessary.

4 Serve with hot crusty bread.

CRISPY ROAST DUCK INFUSED WITH ORANGE

SERVES 4

When choosing a duck for a Western-style recipe look for European breeds. The Thirlmere Poultry brand is one I personally recommend. Raised in the Southern Highlands of New South Wales, the ducks have a good meat to fat ratio as the birds have plenty of exercise. Glenloth Game in Wycheproof, north-west Victoria, also comes very highly recommended. More flavour in the meat has to be a good thing!

1 large free-range duck
500 ml (1 pint) Grand Marnier or other orange
   liqueur
1 tablespoon Eight-Spice Powder (see page 21)
Murray River salt and freshly ground white pepper
250 ml (8½ fl oz) fresh orange juice
250 ml (8½ fl oz) Brown Chicken Stock (see
   page 17)
1 tablespoon cultured butter

PREPARATION

1   This recipe requires you to start the day before to ensure the duck is as dry as possible before it is roasted. The best way to do this is in the dry cool air of a refrigerator. Prepare the duck by removing the wishbone, neck and giblets (reserve all for the sauce). Then dry the skin of the duck with a clean cloth.

2   Put the bird on a chopping board breast side up and using both hands press into the bird until you hear a cracking sound, which is the breastbone breaking. This will ensure the duck cooks more evenly. Splash half the Grand Marnier over the top of the duck and leave it uncovered on a plate in the refrigerator for 8–12 hours or overnight.

TO COMPLETE COOKING

1   Preheat the oven to 230°C (450°F).

2   Using a small skewer, prick the skin of the duck all over, particularly between the legs and the breast. Season the duck by generously rubbing salt, white pepper and the eight-spice powder into the skin.

3   Line a large roasting tray with a sheet of aluminium foil, which will collect excess fat. Put the duck on a roasting rack and into the prepared tray. Cook on the centre shelf of the oven for 1½–2 hours.

4   Three or four times during cooking, remove the tray from the oven and drain the fat from the corner of the tray. This fat is wonderful for roast potatoes so don't throw it away.

5   When the cooking time is up, allow the duck to rest for 20 minutes or so. Meanwhile, place the roasting tray over medium heat and add the duck trim and bones, deglaze with remaining Grand Marnier, reduce by half, add the orange juice and reduce by half, then add the brown chicken stock and bring to the boil, add the butter and whisk in over a high heat. Strain and serve with the carved duck, roast potatoes cooked in duck fat and green beans with garlic (see page 162).

BRAISED RED CABBAGE
WITH PIGEON AND BLUEBERRIES

SERVES 4

A good friend whom I worked with during my Michelin star training showed me how to cook this dish (minus the pigeon) for the daily staff meal. It has a great aromatic smell which draws people to the kitchen. Paddy – thank you for the recipe, I'm sure I have unwittingly changed it over the years, but it still tastes wonderful! Serve with a bottle of aged Bandol from a good year.

2 x 400–600 g (14 oz–1 lb 5 oz) pigeons,
    quartered
Salt and pepper
2 pinches of Eight-Spice Powder (see page 21)
2 tablespoons goose fat
2 onions, finely sliced
2 celery stalks, finely sliced
½ red cabbage, finely sliced or roughly grated
100 g (3½ oz) redcurrant jelly
250 ml (8½ fl oz) red wine
1 punnet blueberries
250 ml (8½ fl oz) Veal Stock (see page 16)

1 Preheat the oven to 160°C (320°F). Rub the pigeons with salt, pepper and the spice powder and set aside.

2 Put the goose fat into a large, heavy-based casserole dish over medium heat; about 30 seconds later add the onion and soften it without letting it colour. Add the celery and cabbage, cook for 2–3 minutes or until the cabbage starts to wilt, stirring constantly. Add the redcurrant jelly, stir into the cabbage.

3 Add the red wine and reduce its volume by half. Add the blueberries and veal stock, bring to the boil and stir. Simmer for a further 1–2 minutes.

4 Remove half the cabbage and place the pigeon pieces in the casserole dish. Put the cabbage back on top. Cover the dish with foil and then the lid. Place in the oven for approximately 2 hours.

5 Remove from the oven and allow to rest for 10 minutes. Taste the cabbage – it should melt in the mouth. Serve with crispy roast potatoes

ROAST RABBIT WITH MUSTARD AND LAVENDER

SERVES 6

French lavender is one of the most underused edible plants in the household garden – a big statement, I know, but it has so many uses in cookery. In appears in the following recipe but I also use it to flavour icings on vanilla sponges or rub into shortbread biscuit recipes and even add it to custards. This recipe is for rabbit lovers; I prefer wild over farmed rabbit, as I find farmed rabbit soft-textured to the point it is mushy and tasteless. Be careful when breaking down the rabbit, as little splinter-type bones can get in the way of enjoying this dish.

1 wild rabbit (800 g–1 kg/about 2 lb)
50 g (2 oz) plain (all purpose) flour
8 sprigs fresh lavender
50 ml (2 fl oz) extra-virgin olive oil
Salt and pepper
Pommes Dauphinoise (see page 156)
125 ml (4 fl oz) Chicken Stock (see page 17)
125 ml (4 fl oz) cream

MUSTARD SAUCE
2 tablespoons olive oil
1 teaspoon chopped shallots
1 teaspoon chopped garlic
1 sprig of thyme
250 ml (8½ fl oz) white wine
250 ml (8½ fl oz) Chicken Stock (see page 17)
    (optional)
100 ml (3½ fl oz) crème fraiche
2 tablespoons Dijon mustard
Salt and pepper

MUSTARD SAUCE

1 Add the olive oil to a medium-sized pan and cook the shallots and garlic until shallots are translucent, then add the thyme and white wine. Reduce until the pan is nearly dry then add the chicken stock and bring to the boil.

2 Add the crème fraiche and Dijon mustard, reduce liquid to desired consistency then season to taste.

RABBIT

1 Remove the legs and forelegs from the carcass. Remove the loins (the part of the back muscles between the end of the ribs and the tail, about 7.5 cm/3 in long) and set aside. Remove belly, kidneys and liver. Remove rib cage.

2 You should end up with two sets of racks, portion these further into 6 even pieces, each piece should have three points.

3 Using a heavy cleaver or knife break the rabbit legs into 2–5 cm (1–2 in) pieces.

4 Put the rabbit pieces into a 4 litre (8 pint) pot and fill with cold water. Add a pinch of salt. Bring to the boil and then simmer for 2–3 minutes. Strain and discard the water. Drain the rabbit well.

5 Toss the rabbit pieces in a bowl of flour to lightly coat them. Separate lavender flowers from stalks.

6 Preheat the oven to 180°C (350°F).

7 Put 12 squares of dauphinoise potatoes into a baking tray, add chicken stock and cream and cover the pan tightly with aluminium foil, bake in the oven for 7 minutes, remove the foil and put back into the oven for another 7 minutes or until golden.

8 As the potatoes warm, heat a heavy frying pan over a medium heat, add the olive oil and sauté the rabbit in 4 or 5 batches. As the pieces turn a golden crisp texture, season with half the lavender flowers and salt and pepper. Remove the pieces and drain on kitchen paper towel.

9 Warm the mustard sauce in a large pot, add the rabbit and toss through the sauce. Season to taste.

10 Put 2 squares of pommes dauphinoise on each plate. Spoon rabbit and sauce over the potatoes, garnish with remaining lavender flowers.

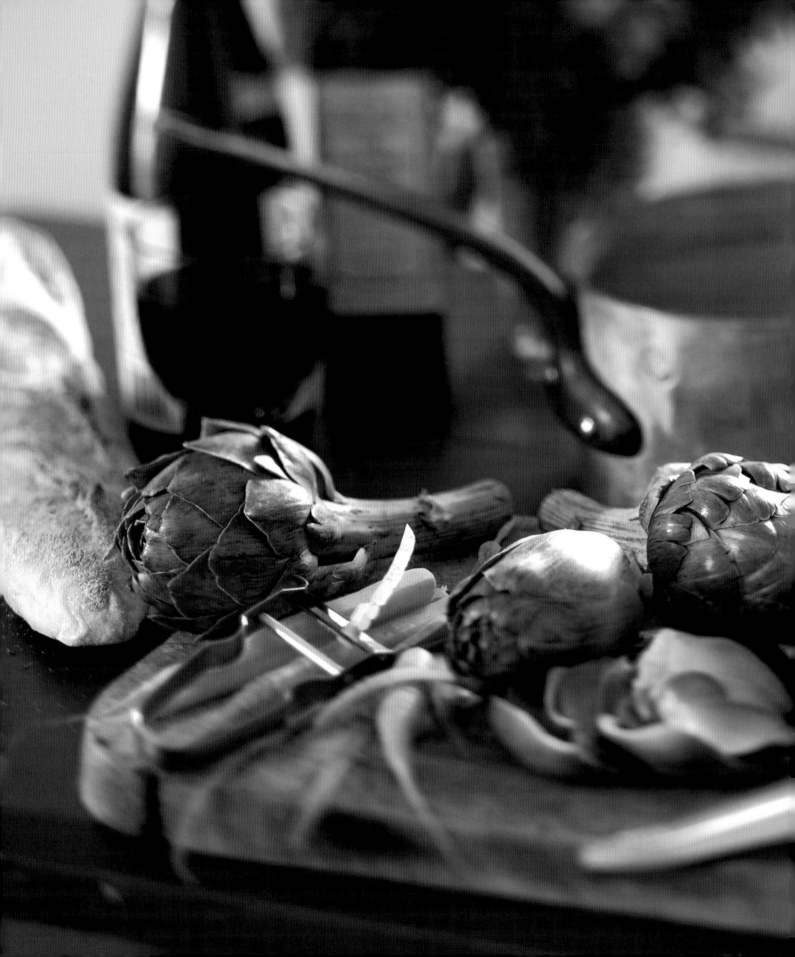

Vegetables

THE PERFECT FRENCH FRIES

SERVES 4

I do not know a single person on this earth who can resist the perfect fried chip! The secret is all in the potato – see the Pantry section, page 12, for information about the best variety of potato to use.

Perfect French fries are sometimes made inadvertently, when you realise just before serving that they are not quite crisp enough and throw them back into the hot oil for another minute: the double cooking improves the finished fries. In my version I also parboil the potatoes before frying. The only disadvantage of the second frying is the fries can become too brown on the outside, and so less appealing to the eye and palate, if allowed to cook too much. For the ultimate gourmand one can replace the vegetable oil with goose, duck or chicken fat – the resultant taste is sensational! Don't fret about the waistline, for if you can afford goose fat then you have more things to worry about, such as managing your finances a little more sensibly!

4 large Sebago potatoes, washed
1 litre (2 pints) vegetable oil
Sea salt

1 Cut the washed potato into 1 cm (½ in) slices. Then cut these slices into 1 cm (½ in) strips. Wash them under cold running until the water runs clear then drain.

2 Fill a large saucepan with water, add a tablespoon of salt. Put the potato into the water, bring to the boil and simmer for 2 minutes.

3 Strain with a large colander or sieve.

4 Heat the oil in a large saucepan (the oil should only fill one-third of the pot). Watch the oil carefully, do not leave it unattended. It should not reach smoking point; it should be 180°C (350°F) for cooking the potatoes.

To test if the oil is at the correct temperature, drop a chip into it and if the chip disappears in a rapid stream of bubbles, then the oil is ready.

5 Cook the fries in batches, a quarter at a time, until golden. Drain on a tray lined with absorbent paper.

6 The fries at this stage may lose their crispiness so before serving, bring the oil back to 180°C and cook the fries until crisp again, about 1 minute. Drain on clean absorbent paper, season well with salt and serve.

POMMES DAUPHINOISE

I used to be under the impression that Dauphinoise was a style named after the heir to the throne of France. In fact, Dauphiné is an ancient region of France covering Savoy to Provence. The wide range of this area, and its diverse cuisine, mean that many ingredients used in French cookery can be cooked à la Dauphinoise.

2 tablespoons olive oil
20 g (¾ oz) butter
4 shallots, diced
5 garlic cloves, finely chopped
1.5 litres (3 pints) pouring cream
6 sprigs of thyme
Salt and pepper
8 large Sebago potatoes, peeled

1 Preheat the oven to 180°C (350°F).

2 Put the olive oil and butter in a heavy-based saucepan on a low heat, and cook the shallots and garlic until shallots are softened.

3 Add the cream and thyme and reduce the liquid by two-thirds. Season well.

4 Using a mandolin, slice the potato into long strips about 3 mm ($^1/_8$ in) thick. Put into a bowl of water.

5 Line the base of a baking tray 30 x 30 cm (12 x 12 in) with silicon paper or greased baking paper.

6 Ladle a small amount of the cream into the tray and arrange a layer of potato slices on top. Repeat cream and potato layers until the tray is half full, making sure to season each layer well. Cover the tray with aluminium foil and bake in the oven for 1½ hours.

7 Remove from the oven, place a weight on top of the foil and chill.

8 Cut into squares 4 x 4 cm (2 x 2 in); 2 pieces are served per portion.

9 Reheat when required.

I particularly like
these potatoes
with roast meats.

PARSLEY POMMES MOUSSELINE

Marco Pierre White's head chef, Robert Reid, showed me this technique. Pommes mousseline is the most decadent of purées and the recipe needs great ingredients, including the butter. Make sure the potato is of the floury variety. Serve this with any of the meat and fish dishes in the book.

2 large Sebago potatoes, peeled
250 g (8 oz) butter, diced
2 tablespoons warm milk
2 teaspoons sea salt

PARSLEY PUREE
1 tablespoon cultured butter
2 shallots, finely diced
250 ml (8½ fl oz) double cream
1 bunch of picked, washed and finely chopped
    curly-leaf or flat-leaf parsley
Salt and freshly ground black pepper

1 For the parsley purée, melt the butter in a heavy-based frying pan, add the shallots and cook for 2–3 minutes or until they are soft and transparent.

2 Add the cream, bring to the boil and reduce, stirring constantly, until thick and smooth. Beat in the parsley and salt and pepper to taste. Set aside.

3 Put the potatoes in cold, salted water, bring to the boil and cook for another 25 minutes. Test with a knife: if it slides in without resistance, the potatoes are cooked. Immediately mash with 90 g (3 oz) of the butter, then mix any visible butter into the potato purée with a wooden spoon.

4 Put the potato purée in a saucepan, add 1 tablespoon of the milk and whisk over low heat for 3–4 minutes.

5 Add the parsley mixture and whisk in until fully incorporated.

6 Add the remaining butter, a quarter at a time, whisking rapidly. If the butter starts to separate, the purée is too hot. Remove from the heat, beat in the remaining l tablespoon milk and whisk like mad to bring it together. When all the butter is incorporated, check the seasoning, add salt if necessary, and serve.

BRAISED LENTILS

Like other legumes, lentils are low in fat and high in protein and fibre, but the biggest advantage is their quick cooking time. Lentils have a mild, often earthy flavour, and they're best if cooked with assertive flavourings. The best, most delicate lentils are the peppery French green ones. These hold their shape well, but take longer to cook than other lentils and are also three times the price. French lentils are grown in the very volcanic, rich soils of the Auvergne region, in particular the Le Puy-en-Velay commune, which has a DOC on producing lentils to specific standards that protect the integrity of this humble pulse. If the 'poor man's caviar' is not available then red lentils (which are much faster to cook but should not be soaked) or split peas are a suitable substitute. By doubling the amount of chicken stock and blending the lentils when cooked you have a fantastic soup.

250 g (9 oz) dried lentil du Puy

1 carrot

1 celery stalk

½ onion

400 ml (13 fl oz) Chicken Stock (see page 17)

2 sprigs of thyme

2 bay leaves

100 g (3½ oz) smoked bacon lardons

25 ml (1 fl oz) olive oil

2 shallots, peeled and finely chopped

1 tablespoon sherry vinegar

10 g (½ oz) cultured butter

1 teaspoon white truffle oil

Salt and pepper

1 Wash the lentils under cold running water, then soak them overnight in cold water in the refrigerator.

2 Make a mirepoix: carefully dice carrot, celery and onion to small, evenly sized cubes and mix together.

3 Drain lentils. Put a heavy-based pot over a low heat, add lentils, 50 g (2 oz) of the mirepoix, the stock and herbs. Bring to a simmer and cook for about 1 hour, until the lentils are soft.

4 Spread the lentil mixture on a flat tray to cool in the refrigerator. Once cold, pick out the mirepoix – but if you are preparing the lentils as a main meal, leave the mirepoix in the lentils.

5 Over medium to high heat, using a heavy-based skillet or pan, sauté the lardons in olive oil until they are golden, then add shallots and cook until they are transparent. Add the cooked lentils, and toss in the pan until warmed through.

6 Build up the heat under the pan to the point where the lentils start to stick to the bottom, then add the sherry vinegar and cook until evaporated. Remove pan from the heat, add the butter and truffle oil, toss through to taste and adjust the seasoning. Serve.

Serve these lentils with any red meat, chicken or fish or even cold with smoked salmon.

GREEN BEANS WITH GARLIC

SERVES 4

These beans are good as an accompaniment to any meat dish. The trick with this dish is not to over- or under-reduce the cream – aim for mayonnaise consistency.

400 g (14 oz) picked green beans (haricot vert)
1 tablespoon cultured butter
2 shallots, finely diced
2 garlic cloves, finely crushed
100 ml (3½ fl oz) Chicken Stock (see page 17)
100 ml (3½ fl oz) double cream
Salt and pepper to taste

1   Blanch the beans in 1 litre (2 pints) boiling water for 2 minutes or until tender, strain and set aside.

2   Melt the butter in a heavy-based frying pan over a low heat. Add the shallots and garlic, stirring until the shallots are tender.

3   Add the chicken stock and turn the heat up to medium. Reduce the stock by three-quarters and add a pinch of salt. Add the cream and then reduce volume by half.

4   Mix through the green beans and season with salt and pepper.

PEA PUREE

SERVES 4

This recipe can be anything you want it to be: soup, a garnish for meat or fish, or, if you add bacon, garlic croutons and onion, you have a light supper. Remember to preserve the green colour by not overcooking the peas. My favourite garnish is to add a poached egg and then to drizzle a few drops of white truffle oil over the egg. Chicken stock can be easily be replaced by a vegetable nage for vegetarians.

1 litre (2 pints) Chicken Stock (see page 17)
2 shallots, sliced
1 garlic clove, crushed
3 sprigs of thyme
500 g (1 lb 2 oz) frozen peas
Salt and pepper

1   Put the chicken stock, shallots, garlic and thyme into a heavy-based saucepan and boil until liquid is reduced by half. Add the peas and simmer for 10 minutes.

2   Remove from the heat, and blitz with a hand blender or a food processor until well blended. Season well.

3   Pass through a fine sieve and set aside until required.

PUMPKIN AND YUZU PUREE

SERVES 4

Pumpkin has so many uses in the kitchen but I cannot go past puréeing it and serving it as a sort of thick soup. I particularly like to season it with the very acidic yuzu juice, to balance the sweetness of the pumpkin. If you want to make a main meal out of this recipe then simply put the hot purée in deep plates and add thinly sliced fresh scallop meat in a layer over the top before you spoon over the yuzu dressing.

2 onions, sliced
2 tablespoons olive oil
3 tablespoons ground cumin
1 tablespoon crushed garlic
4 butternut pumpkins, peeled, deseeded
   and diced
100 g (3½ oz) cultured butter
Salt and freshly ground black pepper
4 teaspoons yuzu juice
4 tablespoons extra-virgin olive oil

1 In a large pot gently cook the onions in the olive oil until soft and then add the cumin and garlic. Gently fry for a few minutes.

2 Add the pumpkin and butter then cover with a lid. Cook over low heat until the pumpkin is easily mashed with a spoon.

3 Purée in a food processor or with a hand-held blender and adjust the seasoning.

4 Mix the yuzu juice and extra-virgin olive oil together. Put the hot purée in individual bowls and spoon the dressing over it.

CURRIED SPINACH

SERVES 4

Curried spinach is a great side dish as well as a delicious meal served with a bowl of steamed rice.

3 tablespoons duck fat
1 onion, finely diced
1 tablespoon medium Madras curry powder
500 ml (1 pint) Chicken Stock (see page 17)
200 ml (7 fl oz) coconut milk
Salt and pepper
250 g (9 oz) spinach, washed
Juice of ½ lemon

1   Sweat the onion in 2 tablespoons of the duck fat in a heavy-based pan over a medium heat.

2   Once the onion is translucent add the curry powder and cook for 30 seconds, ensuring that the curry doesn't catch on the base of the pan.

3   Add the chicken stock, bring to the boil and reduce by half. Add the coconut milk, bring to the boil again and season.

4   Remove from the heat. Blitz until smooth with a hand blender or in a food processor, then set aside in the pot. Put half the sauce in a container and freeze or reserve for another time.

5   Add the remaining duck fat to a heavy-based frying pan over a high heat and add the spinach. Quickly sauté, drain the spinach in a colander and add to the curry sauce. Season with salt, pepper and lemon juice. Serve immediately.

WARM SALAD OF BRUSSELS SPROUTS AND CRISPY FRIED SHALLOTS

SERVES 4

A very simple and quick way of making a vegetable that everybody hates into one that they love. My daughter enjoys picking the near raw leaves up one by one and grazing on them – it makes me realise that being a chef has moments when food reviews really do matter!

250 g (9 oz) brussels sprouts
500 ml (1 pint) vegetable oil or clarified butter
6 banana shallots, thinly sliced
Salt and pepper
2 tablespoons goose fat
2 garlic cloves, crushed
1 tablespoon lilliput capers
1 cup picked flat-leaf parsley leaves

1 Chop the bottoms off the sprouts to free the outer leaves, continue the process until all the leaves are loose. Repeat the process for all the sprouts, discarding the bottoms of the sprouts.

2 Heat the oil to 150°C (300°F) in a 2 litre (4 pint) saucepan, add the shallots in two batches so as not to spill the oil over the side of the pan, cook until golden but not quite crisp. Remove and drain on absorbent paper. Season with salt and leave to the side.

3 Heat a heavy-based frying pan over medium heat, add the goose fat followed by the garlic and quickly sauté the garlic without letting it colour. Add the sprout leaves. Remove from the heat, season and add the crispy shallots, capers and parsley. Toss together gently and serve immediately.

Desserts

CHERRY KUGELHUPF

According to Wikipedia a '"Gugelhupf or Kugelhupf" is a southern German, Austrian, Swiss and Alsatian term for a type of cake. In Croatia and Serbia, it is called *kuglof*. It has the general shape of a torus, like a doughnut.' But to me it is a slightly dry type of cake that marries well with sugar syrup laced with fruity alcohol and macerated fruits, or served with vanilla crème anglaise. There should be two types of plain flour in a serious cook's pantry: a soft flour that has been milled very finely for delicate sponges and cakes, and a hard flour that is best for pasta and crusty breads. All good providores will provide information on purchasing the right flours.

350 g (12 oz) caster (superfine) sugar
350 g (12 oz) unsalted butter
1 vanilla pod, split and scraped
3 whole eggs, beaten
350 g (12 oz) soft cake flour, sieved
15 g (½ oz) baking powder
100 g (3½ oz) maraschino cherries
75 ml (3 fl oz) whole milk
100 g (3½ oz) toasted flaked almonds
Icing (confectioner's) sugar, to dust

SYRUP
75 g (2½ oz) sugar
50 ml (2 fl oz) kirsch
50 ml (2 fl oz) water

1 Preheat oven to 170°C (340°F).

2 Put the sugar, butter and the scraped vanilla seeds in a mixing bowl. Cream together using a spatula or beater on a mixing machine. The mixture should be creamed until all lumps of butter have been removed and it is light and fluffy.

3 Add the eggs, one at a time, continuing to beat the mixture until they are all incorporated.

4 Sieve the flour and baking powder together and fold into the mixture. Add the cherries and milk and fold again until all are incorporated.

5 Put the mixture in a non-stick 25 cm (10 in) diameter kugelhupf mould and flatten it level with the back of a spoon. Bake in the oven for 18–20 minutes.

6 Remove from the oven and leave to rest in the tin for 5 minutes before turning out onto a cooling rack.

7 Put the sugar, kirsch and water into a saucepan and bring to the boil over a medium heat until the sugar has dissolved. Brush the syrup onto the warm sponge using a pastry brush.

8 Top the sponge with toasted flaked almonds and a sprinkle of icing sugar. Serve with fresh cream, crème anglaise or a compote of fruits – or all of these!

This omelette is a dessert best served amongst friends and family at the table; one omelette serves about two people.

OMELETTE ROTHSCHILD

SERVES 4

This omelette was made originally for the well-known Baron de Rothschild, the Jewish banker who was the patron of the famous chef Carême in the 1820s and 1830s, but it is not as well known as other culinary creations named after him. It is an easy recipe: it adds a sweet meringue to an omelette mix which is then filled with a sweet jam and served as a dessert. I have not included a specific fruit to serve with the dish, as you should serve whatever fruit is in season, in summer it could be berries, poached cherries or roast white peaches, while in the colder months maybe ripe pear or oranges – the photograph shows poached orange and tamarillo slices. I learnt to make it with freshly poached apricots but to specify apricots would place a caveat over the dish for nine months of the year – and that would be a pity, as this dessert should be served all year round.

40 g (1½ oz) caster (superfine) sugar
2 eggs, separated
2 teaspoons Grand Marnier
2 teaspoons clarified butter
Poached fruit of choice
Icing (confectioner's) sugar, for dusting

1 Preheat oven to 180°C (350°F).

2 Whisk 30 g (1 oz) of the caster sugar with the egg yolks in a bowl, until the mixture is light and fluffy and draws up in ribbons when the whisk is pulled out of it. Add the Grand Marnier and mix together thoroughly.

3 Whisk egg whites to a stiff peak and then whisk in the remaining sugar.

4 Fold egg yolk mixture and meringue together.

5 In an ovenproof non-stick pan about 12–15 cm (5–6 in) in diameter, heat clarified butter until quite hot. Ladle half the egg mixture into the pan. You must move quickly here and spread the mixture over the surface of the pan.

6 Place the pan in the oven for approximately 1 minute.

7 Take pan out of oven and fill half the surface with some poached, chopped seasonal fruit. Slide the omelette so the omelette folds over itself in the pan.

8 Slide the omelette on a plate, spoon some more poached fruit over and around it, and sprinkle with icing sugar.

9 Repeat to make a second omelette and serve.

FRENCH TOAST WITH BERRIES

French toast is a long-forgotten classic left to the dry environment of 5-star hotel breakfast buffets. Why? My inspiration for this recipe has come from seeing something that should be simple and beautiful turned into something so dry and nasty. If berries are not in season try roasted pears or apples.

250 g (8 oz) fresh raspberries
4 strawberries
50 g (2 oz) blueberries
Juice of ½ lemon
50 g (2 oz) icing (confectioner's) sugar
3 free-range eggs, beaten
50 ml (2 fl oz) whole milk
25 g (1 oz) caster (superfine) sugar
Pinch of cinnamon
Pinch of salt
4 slices brioche, cut 3 cm (1¼ in) thick and crusts
   trimmed off
4 teaspoons clarified butter
2 tablespoons caster sugar
1 quantity Créme Anglaise or 180 g (6 oz)
   clotted cream

CREME ANGLAISE
250 ml (8½ fl oz) milk
Seeds from 1 vanilla bean
100 ml (3½ fl oz) double cream
4 egg yolks
110 g (3½ oz) caster (superfine) sugar

BERRY COMPOTE

1 Wash all the berries in cold water and drain on absorbent paper. Hull the strawberries and cut them in half.

2 Take 200 g (7 oz) of the raspberries and blend them to a purée in a food processor, add the lemon juice and the icing sugar and blend again.

3 Pass the purée through a fine sieve and discard the seeds. Add the remaining berries to the raspberry coulis, mix together and set aside.

CUSTARD

Put the eggs, milk, sugar, cinnamon and salt in a mixing bowl and whisk together by hand for a minute. Set aside.

CREME ANGLAISE

1 Put milk, vanilla seeds and cream into a heavy-based pan and bring to the boil. Remove from heat.

2 Beat yolks and sugar together until pale and creamy. Gently combine egg mixture with milk and return to the stove over a low heat, stirring constantly with a wooden spoon for 3–6 minutes or until it coats the back of the spoon.

3 Strain through a fine sieve into a bowl over ice. Stir occasionally until cool.

TO ASSEMBLE

1 Dip the brioche slices into the custard one at a time until the slices are fully soaked on both sides.

2 Heat a non-stick frying pan over a medium heat until the pan is hot; test the degree of heat by adding a drop of batter in the pan – it should set immediately. Add 1 teaspoon clarified butter and swirl evenly over the pan, do not let it burn.

3 Place a soaked slice of brioche into the pan and cook for 2–3 minutes before turning the slice over and cooking on the other side for the same amount of time. Carefully remove the toast from the pan using a spatula and place it on a warmed plate with caster sugar. Repeat cooking for remaining butter and brioche slices. Roll slices in sugar to coat.

4 Spoon the berry compote equally onto each slice of toast, ensuring all receive the same amount of berries.

5 Warm the créme anglaise gently then spoon onto the berries and serve immediately.

WARM PISTACHIO CUPCAKES

I have decided to part with this recipe because I'm hoping my valuable café clientele can make them at home and possibly try my pastry chefs' other creations, as these cupcakes account for 70 per cent of all the cakes we sell. You might conclude that our other pastries and gateaux are possibly not up to standard … but I know that not to be true! It is a fact that these little moist nutty delights are addictive. You can serve this simple cake as a dessert; after all, I do at Bistro vue. I crumble the cake whilst it's still warm and serve it with frozen and slightly sweetened fromage blanc.

100 g (3½ oz) unsalted butter, softened
85 g (3 oz) caster (superfine) sugar
Pinch of salt
20 g (¾ oz) sweetened pistachio paste
55 g (1 oz) marzipan (minimum 50% nuts)
2 eggs, medium size
100 g (3½ oz) green pistachios, ground
30 g (1 oz) green pistachios, shelled and
    rough chopped
20 ml (¾ fl oz) kirsch
2 drops vanilla essence
30 g (1 oz) semolina
12 patty pan cases
12 whole pistachios, shelled

FONDANT ICING
200 g (7 oz) icing (confectioner's) sugar, sifted
2 tablespoons water
40 g (1½ oz) pistachio paste

1 Preheat a fan-forced oven to 165°C (330°F).

2 For this recipe I recommend using a beater with a paddle attachment. You can make the mixture by hand, though, using a wooden spoon and a metal mixing bowl.

3 Put the butter, sugar, salt, pistachio paste and chopped marzipan into the bowl and beat well until lumps are removed and you have a smooth paste. Add the eggs one at a time, beating continuously and ensuring the mix does not stick to the side of the bowl, until eggs are thoroughly amalgamated.

4 Add the ground and rough chopped nuts and continue to beat. Then beat in the kirsch, vanilla and semolina.

5 Lay out medium-size patty pan cases. Using a piping bag or spoons, place the mix into the cases equally. This should be about 50 g (2 oz) of mixture per case.

6 Put the cakes onto an oven tray and bake for approximately 16 minutes, then remove from the oven and allow to cool on the tray.

7 Make icing: whisk together all ingredients to make a smooth paste. Put it into a clean pan and gently heat, stirring continuously with a wooden spoon, to approximately blood temperature and then spoon over the cakes in equal measure. Place a whole pistachio on top of the warm fondant.

8 Reheat cupcakes in a warm oven for 2 minutes before serving.

CHOCOLATE ORANGE CUSTARDS

Jaffas were my favourite movie sweet when I was growing up so when I discovered during my apprenticeship that chocolate and orange have always been a classic match I was a little disappointed, as I had thought Melbourne had discovered this secret! I got over my disappointment by putting this very simple dish on the menu at Bistro vue. Serve the little pots of custard with orange segments and some sort of crispy wafer or biscuit. You will need a cooking thermometer for the recipe.

160 ml (6 fl oz) milk
160 ml (6 fl oz) cream
40 ml (1½ fl oz) orange juice
20 ml (¾ fl oz) Grand Marnier
2 oranges, juiced and zested
40 g (1½ oz) sugar
2 large eggs
4 large egg yolks
100 g (3½ oz) milk couverture chocolate pieces
140 g (5 oz) dark coverture chocolate pieces
Additional zest of 1 orange, for garnish

* NOTE *
It is best to zest the oranges with a microplane as this extracts all the natural oils that are in the zest and gives a great aroma to the custard.

1 Put the milk, cream, orange juice, Grand Marnier, orange zest and half the sugar in a heavy-based saucepan and bring to a simmer. Remove from the heat, set aside and leave to infuse for 10–15 minutes.

2 Meanwhile whisk the eggs and egg yolks with the remaining sugar.

3 Bring the infused liquid to a simmer again and then pour through a fine sieve into the whisked egg yolks. The sieve will catch the zest, which can be discarded.

4 Whisk until the egg mixture has dissolved into the infused liquid.

5 Clean the saucepan and return the mixture to the pan, and heat over a low to medium heat until liquid reaches 78°C (172°F), using a cooking thermometer, stirring constantly (at this point the custard will *lightly* coat the back of a wooden spoon). Put the chocolate pieces into a mixing bowl.

6 Once the custard has reached the required temperature, pour it over the chocolate buttons and mix with a spatula until you get a really rich and homogenised liquid.

7 Pour into ramekins and set in the refrigerator for at least 1 hour. If there are air bubbles tap ramekins lightly on the bench top. They should have a decadent look about them and be very dark in appearance.

8 To serve, garnish tops with a pinch or two of fine orange zest.

CAFE VUE RASPBERRY TART

Whoever invented frangipane was a genius! It is served in every reputable pastry shop, restaurant and café around the globe and it can transform a simple afternoon tea idea into an elaborate dessert to finish a great meal. The base frangipane can be topped with any fresh fruit, or even macerated fruits such as prunes soaked in Armagnac. A simple tip when using macerated fruits is to place them before baking, by gently pushing them into the frangipane, then when the tart or tartlets are baked glaze them with some melted raspberry or apricot jam. Serve this with a cold glass of Muscat de Beaumes de Venise.

SWEET PASTRY
250 g (9 oz) cultured butter at room
   temperature, diced
215 g (7½ oz) caster (superfine) sugar
2 medium eggs
Pinch of salt
475 g (1 lb 1 oz) plain (all purpose) flour

FRANGIPANE
250 g (9 oz) cultured butter at room
   temperature, diced
250 g (9 oz) caster (superfine) sugar
4 eggs, beaten
250 g (9 oz) ground almonds
75 g (2½ oz) plain (all purpose) flour, sifted

RASPBERRY CREME CHANTILLY
250 ml (8½ fl oz) thickened cream
25 g (1 oz) icing (confectioner's) sugar, sifted,
   and extra for dusting
1 vanilla pod (optional)
200 g (7 oz) fresh raspberries

* Note *
Make the pastry mix and frangipane filling first and rest them in the refrigerator for at least 2 hours before using. They will both keep refrigerated for a week and any leftovers can be frozen.

PASTRY

1 Using the paddle attachment of a mixer on medium speed, cream butter and caster sugar together until pale and fluffy. Slowly incorporate eggs one at the time, to prevent curdling. Add salt and flour and mix on slow speed until just combined. Over-mixing at this stage will make the dough hard to work due to activating the gluten in the flour.

2 Divide into two portions, about two-thirds and one-third respectively, wrap in cling film and rest in the refrigerator until needed.

FRANGIPANE

Using the paddle attachment of a mixer on medium speed, cream butter and caster sugar together until pale and fluffy. Slowly incorporate the eggs one at a time, to prevent curdling. Add ground almonds and flour, mix until combined.

TART

1 Preheat the oven to 200°C (400°F).

2 To make the tartlets you will need all the pastry. To make the large tart you will only need about two-thirds and can store the remaining pastry in the freezer. Gently knead pastry to a workable temperature and consistency. Using a rolling pin and a light dusting of flour, roll to a thickness of 3 mm ($^1/_8$ in).

3 Brush a 30 cm (12 in) tart tin or 12 small tart moulds with clarified butter or vegetable oil. Line the tin with the dough working from the centre out, ensuring it is evenly distributed and of an appropriate thickness; if making tartlets, cut circles of pastry using a 10 cm (4 in) cutter and line moulds. Trim excess pastry with a sharp knife.

4 Place the frangipane mix into a piping bag and fill the pastry up to 2.5 mm ($^1/_8$ in) from the top. Bake the tartlets for 12 minutes; for the larger tart you will need to adjust the cooking time to 15–20 minutes or until golden brown.

5 Leave to cool in the tin on a wire rack for about 30 minutes. Gently remove the tart from the tin and leave to cool for a further 30 minutes.

TO FINISH

1 Make the crème chantilly: in a mixing bowl add the icing sugar to the cream, then scrape the seeds of the vanilla pod into the mixture. Whip until cream is just firm enough to work with.

2 Top tart or tartlets with the whipped cream and fresh raspberries, and finish with a generous dusting of icing sugar.

APPLE DUMPLINGS

This is my Mum's recipe – one that I enjoyed so much as a young boy. The soft gooey and doughy texture of the dumplings combined with the golden syrup makes for a heavenly and simple dessert.

125 g (4 oz) self-raising flour (cake flour with
 1½ teaspoons baking powder added)
2 teaspoons caster (superfine) sugar
60 g (2 oz) cultured butter at room temperature,
 diced
2 tablespoons water
1 golden delicious apple
Pinch of Eight-Spice Powder (see page 21)
 (or a pinch each of cinnamon and nutmeg)

SAUCE
225 g (8 oz) brown sugar
1 tablespoon golden syrup
375 ml (12 fl oz) water
30 g (1 oz) unsalted butter

1 Preheat the oven to 160°C (320°F).

2 Combine the flour, sugar, butter and water in a mixer or food processor. Use the pulse mechanism until it has formed a dough or use your hands to bring it together. Rest the dough for 20 minutes.

3 Meanwhile, peel, core and cut the apple lengthways into eighths. Season apple with the spice mix.

4 Divide the dough into 8 pieces and roll out to rough circles 3–4 mm (¼ in) thick. Place a piece of apple on each and wrap the dough around the apple, sealing well at the top. Ensure that the pastry is well sealed all around the apple so that the apple will steam inside whilst the pastry cooks.

5 To make the sauce, combine all the ingredients and bring to the boil in a small saucepan. Pour the sauce into a shallow casserole dish (around 22 cm/8 in diameter and 5–6 cm/2 in deep). Place the dumplings on the sauce and bake in oven for approximately 30 minutes or until golden and the apples are cooked.

6 Allow to cool for 5–10 minutes and serve with vanilla ice-cream, spooning the sauce over the top.

Clafoutis is always served hot and many French like to eat it for a sweet breakfast.

RUM AND RAISIN CLAFOUTIS

Clafoutis is a dessert of fruit in batter – it's a delicious French country dish from the rural Limousin region of central France. The name clafoutis comes from the ancient Occitan dialect verb *clafir*, 'to fill'. Traditionally clafoutis is made with cherries, which are unpitted as the stones are believed to add flavour. However, I find cherries a little one-dimensional in such a simple dish, and here is my interpretation of this dessert. Any fruit may be used, just be sure that if you decide to use a hard fruit to cook or poach it first as the fruit will not have enough baking time in the oven.

500 g (1 lb 2 oz) raisins (if there are too many raisins for the clafoutis they are delicious served with cheese)
750 ml (25 fl oz) dark Caribbean rum
250 ml (8½ fl oz) double cream
2 tablespoons almond meal
50 g (2 oz) caster (superfine) sugar
2 medium eggs
Icing (confectioner's) sugar
Vanilla ice-cream

1 Pour the rum over the raisins and leave to macerate overnight in an airtight container. The soaked raisins may be kept for up to 3 months.

2 The following day, strain off the rum and discard it, reserving the raisins.

3 Preheat the oven to 165°C (330°F).

4 Grease 4 individual large ramekin dishes with butter. Place evenly spaced on a suitable oven tray and set aside.

5 Put cream, almond meal, caster sugar, eggs and most of the raisins – reserving about 2 tablespoons – into a mixing bowl and blend with a hand blender to a thick, incorporated batter. Now gently fold the extra raisins into the mix.

6 Spoon into the individual baking dishes. Cover each ramekin with aluminium foil and bake in the oven for 15 minutes.

7 Dust with icing sugar and serve immediately with vanilla ice-cream.

HONEYCOMB SOUFFLE

This is the perfect dessert for the serious sweet tooth! I love it because it combines two very different yet traditional techniques – the confectioner's art of making honeycomb and the pastry chef's specialty of soufflé making.

HONEYCOMB
200 g (7 oz) caster (superfine) sugar
40 g (1½ oz) honey
75 g (2½ oz) liquid glucose
35 ml (1½ fl oz) water
10 g (⅓ oz) bicarbonate of soda

CREME PATISSIERE
600 ml (20 fl oz) milk
1 vanilla bean, seeds scraped out and reserved
8 egg yolks
1 egg
120 g (4 oz) caster (superfine) sugar
40 g (1½ oz) cornflour (cornstarch)
40 g (1½ oz) plain (all purpose) flour

SOUFFLE
40 g (1½ oz) unsalted butter, softened
4 egg whites
100 g (3½ oz) caster (superfine) sugar
140 g (5 oz) Crème Pâtissière

HONEYCOMB

1 Put sugar, honey, glucose and water in a heavy-based saucepan and gently bring to the boil. Increase the heat and when the caramel reaches 155°C (310°F) whisk in the bicarbonate of soda. (If you don't have a sugar thermometer, 155°C is the hard crack stage, when the liquid has all but evaporated and a drop of syrup put into iced water will form brittle threads.)

2 Pour into a greased tin and allow to set. Once set, crush it in a mortar and pestle or with a rolling pin (put honeycomb in a plastic bag first if using the rolling pin).

CREME PATISSIERE

1 Bring the milk and the vanilla bean and its seeds to the boil in a heavy-based saucepan. Remove from heat.

2 Put the yolks, whole egg, sugar and the flours into a mixer and using the paddle attachment beat thoroughly until pale and smooth.

3 Remove vanilla pod from milk and mix a third of the milk into the egg mixture. Return all of this mix into the pan with the remaining vanilla milk and stir continuously over a medium heat until it has begun to thicken and the floury taste has disappeared.

4 Bring to the boil, and when the mixture has boiled for a few seconds transfer it back into the food processor and beat until cold.

5 Store in the refrigerator until needed.

SOUFFLE

1 Preheat oven to 180°C (350°F).

2 Brush 4 individual soufflé moulds with the unsalted butter. Line the moulds with the crushed honeycomb.

3 Whisk the egg whites with the sugar to a stiff meringue. Beat a third of the meringue into the crème pâtissière. Then fold the remaining meringue gently into the mixture.

4 Carefully fill the moulds with the soufflé mix. Cook for 8–10 minutes in the oven and serve immediately.

The honeycomb ingredients
will make more than is needed
for the soufflé, but you can
give leftovers to the kids.

ROQUEFORT WITH CHOCOLATE SPONGE

SERVES 6

You may be thinking that the combination of chocolate and blue cheese is strange – and you would be correct. Credit for this combination must go to Heston Blumenthal of The Fat Duck in England, as a few years ago I ate a blue cheese chocolate that he had cooked; it was the inspiration for this simple yet refined dish. There will be leftover chocolate sponge, but I'm sure you can put it to good use.

40 g (1½ oz) unsalted butter, plus a little extra, softened, for greasing tin

3 tablespoons cocoa powder, for tin

140 g (5 oz) dark coverture chocolate (66% cocoa solids)

45 ml (1½ fl oz) espresso coffee

Additional 1 tablespoon cocoa powder

3 eggs, separated

75 g (2½ oz) caster (superfine) sugar

300 g (10½ oz) Roquefort cheese

1 Preheat a fan-forced oven to 180°C (350°F), or a non-fan-forced oven to 200°C (400°F).

2 Brush a square cake tin – 18 x 18 cm, 6 cm deep (7 x 7 in, 2½ in deep) – with the softened butter and then coat it with the 3 tablespoons of cocoa powder, tapping the tin to ensure it is evenly coated.

3 In a heavy-based saucepan melt the chocolate and the butter together, remove from the heat and add coffee, cocoa powder and egg yolks.

4 Whisk the egg whites with the sugar to form a soft, peaked meringue and fold into the chocolate mixture.

5 Pour the mix into the prepared tin and bake for approximately 15 minutes or until a skewer inserted into the cake comes out clean. Leave the sponge to cool in the tin for 10 minutes before turning out onto a cake rack.

6 Cool sponge and then cut into squares of approximately 4 x 4 cm (2 x 2 in).

7 Serve each portion of cake with a piece of Roquefort cheese, cut into a matching square of 4 x 4 cm (2 x 2 in).

BRIE WITH ROAST WALNUTS, CELERY AND APPLE   SERVES 4

Cheese is becoming a very popular way of finishing a meal, mainly because it is easy to prepare, healthier than many desserts, and suits those with dietary problems such as gluten intolerance. If time is on your side peel the walnuts by blanching them in milk and then peeling away the skin using a small utility knife. Ripe brie should smell earthy, nearly truffle-like, and the outer mould should look creamy. Three bries I recommend are Coulommiers, brie de Nangis and brie de Meaux.

200 g (7 oz) wedge of ripe brie
1 golden delicious apple, peeled and cored
1 celery stalk, peeled
20 walnut halves
Murray River salt
1 tablespoon walnut oil

1 Allow brie to come to room temperature if it has been in the refrigerator. Cut the brie into four even squares or wedges and place each piece in the centre of a plate.

2 Cut the apple into matchstick-size pieces. Cut the celery into similar-sized pieces. Set both aside.

3 Put the walnuts into a heavy-based skillet or frying pan over a medium heat and toast, tossing the walnuts around to ensure an even toasting. Season the nuts with salt.

4 Add the apple and celery and toss these through with the walnuts, then remove from the heat. Add the walnut oil and toss thoroughly again.

5 Carefully spoon the warm salad over each piece of brie, positioning it on top without allowing the salad to fall off the sides and making the plate look scattered. Serve immediately.

Acknowledgments

I would like to thank the following people for their support, for without their assistance this book would not have been possible: Ryan Clift, Anna Curry and all the staff at Vue de monde. Simon Griffiths and Fiona Hammond for the beautiful photography. Clare Coney and all the team at Simon & Schuster for their guidance. Callum Fraser for providing 'the studio'. And Ben and Bridie Bennett for their endless running around and invaluable assistance, along with Andrew Gourlay, in bringing Bistro Vue to life.

Index